The Life of

St. Philip Neri

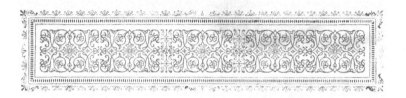

The Life of St. Philip Neri

𝕬postle of 𝕽ome

and the

Founder of the Congregation of the Oratory

by
Mrs. Anne Hope
Author of "The Early Martyrs"

Originally published by:

LONDON:
BURNS AND LAMBERT,
MDCCCLIX

Reprinted by
𝕸ediatrix 𝕻ress
MMXV

ISBN: 9780692381250

Reprinted from the 1859 edition
published by Burns and Lambert

All images are public domain.

Table of Contents

Editor's Preface to the Mediatrix Press Edition

It is a great pleasure to offer this excellent work on St. Philip Neri, which is filled with devotion and love for the saint, as well as a faithful account of his miracles. In this reprinted edition, we have taken great pains to retain the British spelling and punctuation of the original, only changing it where absolutely necessary for stylistic reasons or changes in the meaning of the language, which would lend a different interpretation to what the words meant in the author's time. Thankfully these instances were but a few. We have also taken pains to translate the direct quotes from Latin or Italian which appear in the text to aid the modern reader, unless the meaning is painfully obvious.

St. Philip Neri stands at a crossroads of history. . . he is truly the saint of the 16th century, known to, friend of and confessor to many popes, saints and religious founders. This work tells the story of a man who loved Jesus so much he despised everything else. If there is anything the 21st century needs, it is the testimony of a man who loved, and by loving, changed everything around him.

Although he was the quintessential saint of the 16th century, he is just as much the saint of our time, whose mild manner, overflowing charity, and unfailing devotion to Jesus Christ should inspire every reader to answer that call, which the Church has always affirmed is not merely for religious, or priests, but for every man, to become great saints, emptied of the spirit of the world, filled with the love of Christ and His Church.

Ryan Grant
Post Falls, ID
2015

Author's Protestation

The materials for this work have been taken from Father Antonio Gallonio's Life of St. Philip, and from the edition of Bacci's Life of St. Philip, with the additions by a Father of the Venetian Oratory, published at Florence, A.D. 1851; and all the facts have been verified on oath at the process of canonization.

THE LIFE OF ST. PHILIP NERI

CHAPTER I

 N STUDYING the lives of the saints no circumstance is more calculated to excite our admiration than the infinite variety which appears in them. While all of them can be plainly seen to have been moulded into the same Divine image by the same Spirit, yet of each it may be said with the Church, "*Non est inventus similis illi.*"[1]

The distinctive characteristic of St. Philip Neri, who is the subject of the following pages, was a most wonderful union with God amidst a seemingly ordinary outward life, spent in the labours of the apostolic vocation. His sphere was not the cloister, but the world; his position was that of a secular priest; he filled no high office of dignity, and underwent no extraordinary outward sufferings; and yet, without quitting this humble vocation, he attained to such extraordinary perfection in the practice of virtue, and to such a high state of union with God, while at the same time he exerted such a remarkable influence on all around him, that the Church has conferred on him the singular distinction of sharing with the apostolic princes the title of Apostle of Rome.

St. Philip was born in Florence, on the 21st July, A.D. 1515, and was baptized by the name of Filippo Romolo, in the Church of St. John Baptist. His father was Francesco Neri, and his mother, Lucrezia, daughter of Antonio d'Andrea and Lena Soldi, both of them persons of good family, and bearing a high character for piety and virtue. They had four children; two daughters, Catherine and

---

[1] "One like him has never been discovered." -Editor

Elizabeth, and two sons, Antonio and Philip, the former of whom died in his childhood.

Philip was a handsome and intelligent child, with a sweet temper and winning manner, which endeared him to all who saw him. From his earliest childhood he was remarkable for his obedience to his father and mother, and after his mother's death, to his father's stepmother;[2] so that if they told him to stay in any place, he would remain there for hours, and could by no means be induced to quit it till he had their express permission to do so. He never in any way incurred his father's displeasure, except once, when he gave his sister Catherine a slight push, because she would persist in interrupting him and his other sister while they were reading the Psalms together; and on this occasion, his father having reproved him, he was so filled with sorrow and compunction, that he wept bitterly. His little companions generally called him Good Pippo, for he was always cheerful, and so sweet-tempered that it seemed impossible to make him angry.

When he was between eight and nine years of age he had a very narrow escape of his life; for, having thoughtlessly jumped on the back of a donkey which was standing in the courtyard, they both fell down some steps into a cellar, the donkey falling on him in such a way that only one of his arms was visible. The terrified servants ran to his assistance, expecting to find him dead; but, to their great surprise, they drew him forth safe and sound, without having received the slightest injury.

As soon as he reached a proper age, his parents placed

---

[2] Some writers have called this lady Philip's stepmother: but the Florentine editor has proved, by reference to the genealogical tree of the family, that Francesco Neri was not twice married, but his father was; whence it follows that the lady in question was Francesco's stepmother, and not Philip's.

him to study Latin and rhetoric, under the best masters in Florence. He made such rapid progress in his studies that he quickly outstripped his companions, while at the same time he won the love and esteem of both his masters and his school-fellows, by the purity and modesty of his conduct, and by his gentle temper, so that he was commonly known among them by the name of Good Philip.

But, besides this general sweetness and amiability, Philip seemed from his earliest years to be filled with the love of God; and even at this period his devotion had the same simple and solid character as in after years. Instead of occupying himself with the ordinary childish amusement of dressing altars and images, he spent his time in praying, repeating psalms, and listening to the word of God; and so far from talking about wishing to be a priest, or to enter religion, he carefully shunned every kind of ostentation, and kept secret the aspirations with which God favoured him. Prayer was his resource in all his little troubles, and God rewarded his simple faith by always granting his childish petitions. Having once dropped a gold chain in the street, he had recourse to prayer, and instantly found it; and on another occasion he recovered, by the same means, a bundle of clothes which he had inadvertently let fall.

His greatest recreation was to visit the churches, that of St. Mark, which belonged to the Dominicans, being his favourite resort. In after years he used to say to the Dominicans at Rome, "Whatever good there was in me in my youth, I owe to your fathers at St. Mark's." He also derived great profit from the preaching of Fra. Baldolini, of the order of Umiliati, who came to Florence when he was eleven years old.

He early conceived a great desire to suffer with Jesus; but he contented himself at first with receiving joyfully the ordinary sufferings which God sent him. Thus, when he was between fifteen and sixteen, he had a severe attack of fever; but, so far from complaining, he went about as usual with a bright and happy countenance till at last the sister of his father's stepmother perceived that he was ill, and gave him the necessary remedies. He did not affect any extraordinary love of poverty, but his contempt for wealth and worldly rank betrayed itself in many trifling ways. A great quantity of his clothes having been burnt, he was not the least discomposed, but plainly showed his indifference to the loss. And on another occasion, the genealogical tree of his pedigree being shown him, he indignantly seized it, and tore it to pieces, having no other ambition than to see his name inscribed in the Book of Life.

Tradition tells us, that though the Holy Child of Nazareth spoke and acted like other children, yet the neighbours used to come and see Him, saying, that whatever might be their sorrow or their anxiety, the mere sight of Mary's child sufficed to fill their hearts with peace. In this respect Philip followed the holy model set before him. For though there was nothing very remarkable in his words or actions, yet there breathed around him such an atmosphere of purity and joy, that all who knew him felt there was in him something more than met the eye; so that when, in after years, there came to Florence reports of his great sanctity, one of his relatives replied, "I do not wonder at it, for I remember well what he was as a youth among us."

CHAPTER II

Weached the age of sixteen, the question naturally arose, what was to be his future profession? Francesco Neri had a cousin who was settled in business at St. Germano, in the kingdom of Naples, and who, having no children, might be naturally expected to leave his wealth to Francesco's family. Francesco, therefore, determined to send Philip to him, hoping that, by application to business he might recommend himself to his cousin's favour, and eventually become his heir. Few things could have been more distasteful to Philip than the bustle of commerce and the pursuit of wealth; but, notwithstanding, he applied himself so diligently to his new duties, that he quickly won his cousin's affection, and the old man determined to make him his heir.

But though Philip had bowed to his father's wishes, he had not laid aside his secret aspirations, nor his habits of prayer. While the best portion of his day was given to business, his hours of recreation were devoted to God. The town of St. Germano stands near the foot of a mountain, in which are three great yawning chasms, rending it from its summit to its base, and caused, as tradition says, by the earthquake which marked the hour of our Lord's death. In the largest of these, the Benedictine monks of Monte Cassino have built a small chapel, to which Philip used to retire as soon as he was released from his other duties; and here, kneeling before the crucifix, he would spend hour after hour meditating on the Passion, and praying most fervently to be taught how to carry out the aspirations after a better life, with which the Holy Spirit had filled his heart. Thus he continued to pray day after day and night after night, till at last God plainly showed him what his next step was to be; and just at the time when his cousin had resolved to make him his heir, he himself had come to the determination of giving up home, and family, and earthly possessions, and going out alone into the world, in order to be at liberty to serve God more freely and unreservedly. When he communicated his resolution to his cousin, the old man was very much grieved, and used every means to turn him from his purpose; at one time tempting him by the offer of all his wealth, then urging on him his duty to his family, and finally appealing to his affectionate heart by reminding him of his own claims to his gratitude. But though Philip was touched by his cousin's affection, he had a higher prize before him, and was not to be turned from its pursuit; and so, thanking him in brief and modest terms, he said that, "as to the many favours he had received from him, he should never forget them; but for the rest, he valued his affectionate intention more than his advice." Then, without waiting to inform his father of his resolution, he took leave of his cousin and of St. Germano, and, turning his back on all that could tempt him away from the simple love of God, he bent his steps to Rome.

CHAPTER III

 n the year 1533 Philip entered Rome, penniless and a stranger, and from that day till his death, sixty-two years after, he never quitted it. He found a home with Galeotto Caccia, a Florentine gentleman, who, being struck with his modest demeanour and destitute condition, offered him a small room in his house, and assigned him an annual allowance of flour. In return for this kindness, Philip took charge of Galeotto's two little sons, instructing them in all that was suited to their years, and training them in habits of purity and almost angelic virtue.

Though Philip lived for many years under Galeotto Caccia's roof, he formed no part of the family, but led a life almost as solitary and abstemious as if he had been in the desert. His food was a little loaf, which he daily fetched from the baker's in exchange for his annual allowance of flour; his only drink was water; and though the servants often laid by for him a portion from the family meal, he always declined their kindness, and, going down to the courtyard, would seat himself beside the well, and dine off bread and water, flavoured occasionally with a few herbs or olives. Even of this frugal diet he ate sparingly, never taking more than one meal in the day, and sometimes passing three whole days without food. His little room contained no other furniture than his bed, and a rope across it, on which he hung his clothes. His leisure time was given to prayer, and, as the days were too short to satisfy the cravings of his loving heart, he was in the habit of devoting whole nights to it.

After he had been nearly two years in Rome, he was led, A.D. 1534, to study theology and philosophy. He studied theology in the school of the Augustinian Fathers, and philosophy under Alfonso Ferro and Cæsar Jacomelli, both of whom were then in high repute in Rome. He was soon acknowledged to hold the first place among his fellow-students; and he laid at this time such a solid foundation of theological knowledge, that even when he was an old man, he would discuss the deepest theological questions with the first scholars of the day, with the same correctness and readiness as if he had but just quitted the schools. He also showed great taste for both Latin and Italian poetry, and wrote Italian verse with the greatest facility; but, as his humility led him to burn all his papers before his death, none of his poetical compositions now remain, except three sonnets, the originals of which are carefully preserved in the Roman Oratory.

Notwithstanding his retiring habits, his talents and gentle demeanour quickly attracted the notice of his masters; and when, in course of time, they discovered the character of his life, and remarked the unobtrusive humility and perseverance with which he practised the highest virtues, they gave him the name of Filippo Buono, the title which he had won in his childhood in his native town thus following him in his manhood to the great city in which he was a stranger.

His studies, however, were not allowed to interfere with his spiritual exercises. The hours which other students gave to recreation, he devoted to works of charity, visiting the sick in the hospitals, or catechizing the beggars who thronged the porticos of St. Peter's and St. John Lateran. And when evening closed in, he would seek some unfrequented church, where he would be least liable to interruption; and, seating himself in a retired nook, he would turn to the Gospels and the Lives of the Saints, which he was never tired of reading, or falling on his knees, he would raise his mind to the contemplation of heavenly things; and, as hour after hour passed away, there he would remain immovable, pouring out his fervent affections in prayer, sighing to be filled with the Holy Spirit, and earnestly entreating to be taught how to follow Jesus in the hidden way of lowliness, contempt, and suffering. He had such facility in prayer that he had no need to excite his devotion by discursive meditation, but, on the contrary, was obliged to repress the fervour with which he was constantly inflamed. The mere sight of a crucifix would often cause him to burst into tears, insomuch that, when he was in the schools, he found it very difficult to attend to the lectures, because there happened to hang before him a beautiful crucifix, which filled him with such tender emotions that every time he cast his eyes on it he began to sigh and weep.

Three years passed in this way, and at the end of that time Philip came to the resolution of quitting the schools, selling his books for the benefit of the poor, and giving himself up entirely to the acquisition of that wisdom which is to be found only at the foot of the crucifix. This resolution he carried into effect about the close of the year 1537.

Solitary as Philip's life had hitherto been, he now withdrew into a deeper retirement. For the first year after he gave up his studies he may be said to have lived in absolute solitude, a hermit in the centre of Rome. Though Galeotto Caccia's house still continued to be his home, he was seldom to be found there. During the day he sought out the least frequented churches wherein to pray, and, as evening drew on, he would go on a pilgrimage to the seven ancient Basilicas, in one or other of which he would spend the night. Sometimes it would happen that he found the church closed, and then he might be seen through the livelong night in the portico, reading by the light of the moon, for he was too poor to afford himself a taper; or, kneeling before the closed door, watching eagerly for the moment when it should be opened, and he should be admitted to the presence of his Lord. At the same time he practised the most severe mortification. He avoided society, and observed the strictest silence; he lived on dry bread, flavoured occasionally with a few herbs; he slept little, and always on the bare ground; he disciplined himself with small chains almost every day and, in order to leave his mind more free for the fervent contemplation of divine things, he carefully avoided whatever could in any way afford pleasure or consolation to his human nature.

But still he found not in unfrequented churches, whether by day or by night, the deep solitude for which his heart was yearning. At last he bethought himself of the catacombs, where none would cross his path, or witness the emotions which often overcame him. From this time the Catacomb of St. Calixtus became his favourite haunt; and there, surrounded by the bones of the martyrs, those eloquent monuments of the early Church's love, he would apply his whole soul to the contemplation of the subjects most calculated to inflame his heart with the same burning love. It is impossible to tell what passed between his soul and God during these retreats; but he was so carried away by his devotion that he would often remain for forty hours in uninterrupted prayer, and occasionally he would stay underground for three whole days and nights without either eating or drinking.

The love of God has, however, such an expansive character, that it cannot long be pent up in the human breast; but, like a subterranean fire, will force for itself a vent into the free air, where it may find food whereon to feed. The same love which had driven Philip down into the very bowels of the earth, to meditate on the infinite love and sufferings of Jesus, would not let him rest there, but drove him back into the busy haunts of men to seek and save those for whom Jesus had shed His Precious Blood; and accordingly in the year 1538, he was once more to be seen in the most frequented thoroughfares, in the shops, in the porticos of churches, in the hospitals—in fact, wherever sinners were to be found, discoursing in his own sweet, winning way with persons of all classes.

He turned his attention especially to the reformation of the young men in the drapers' shops, whom he would often address with the words, "Well, brothers, when shall we begin to lead a good life?" His manner was so attractive that none could resist its fascination; and these thoughtless youths, who would have turned in scorn from severe or grave rebuke, were lured on by his gentle and cheerful tone to listen to his exhortations, and thus many of them were completely won to the service of God.

It must not be supposed that Philip's great fervour procured him an exemption from temptation. He was subject to all the temptations common to youth; but he was always so careful to avoid whatever might prove an occasion of sin, that he easily repelled them. At this time, and even for many years after he became a priest, he avoided the society of women, and would not allow his zeal for their conversion to lead him into familiar discourse with them. Once, soon after he came to Rome, he was accosted as he was leaving St. Peter's by some wicked men, who wished to lead him into sin; but he answered them in a far different tone, speaking to them about heavenly things with such supernatural power, that they were struck with remorse and confessed their sorrow for their late sinful intentions. Once, too, as he was passing the Coliseum, the devil appeared to him in the form of a naked figure; and on another occasion, when he happened to be alone at night in the street called Capo di Bore, three devils met him, and tried to frighten him. But on these, and all similar occasions Philip came off victorious; for he was so constantly on his guard, that as soon as he was attacked he was aware of the danger, and having instant recourse to prayer, he quickly conquered the tempter, under whatever form he assailed him.

CHAPTER IV

 LEVEN YEARS had now elapsed since Philip had broken through all earthly ties, and it did not yet appear that he had made this sacrifice for any very definite or adequate object. One less loving and less dead to self might have been tempted to doubt whether, after all, he had not mistaken the will of God; and it is no reproach to Philip to suppose that this long delay was a trial to him. But at last, after eleven long years of patient hope and expectation, he had his reward.

Through his whole life Philip had a special devotion to the Third Person of the Blessed Trinity. As a layman, he was in the habit of praying daily for the gifts and graces of the Holy Spirit; and when he came to be a priest, he never omitted to use the collect beginning with, "*Deus cui omne cor patet,*"[3] whenever the rubrics left him at liberty to do so. In the year 1544, shortly before Pentecost, he was as usual in the catacomb, praying with more than ordinary fervour to be filled with the Holy Spirit, when suddenly there appeared to him a luminous sphere, like a globe of fire, which, entering his lips, passed into his breast. At the same moment he felt within him a flame of rapturous love. It seemed to glow like a material fire, so that, unable to bear the heat which consumed him, he threw himself on the ground and tore open his dress. After a time, the heat abating, he arose, when an unusual joy thrilled through his soul, while at the same time his whole body was agitated by a strange palpitation; and as he placed his hand on his side just over his heart, he felt that it was swollen, though it did not give

---

[3] God, to Whom every heart is open. -Editor

him the slightest pain.

During the remainder of his life this palpitation continued, and this tumour was apparent. The first physicians in Rome prescribed for the palpitation, which gave rise to frequent fits of illness, but they came to the conclusion that it was supernatural; and after his death the cause of the swelling was discovered, two of his ribs being found to be broken, and raised up so as to leave an open space between the fractured ends.

This supernatural palpitation was not constant, but took place only when Philip was engaged in spiritual acts, such as saying Mass, or giving Absolution or Holy Communion, or praying, or speaking on spiritual subjects. It was so violent that his heart seemed about to jump out of his breast; it shook the seat on which he sat, or the bed on which he lay, or the steps of the altar at which he was saying Mass and at times even the room in which he was vibrated as with an earthquake. Several of his penitents affirmed that when he pressed them, as was his custom, to his breast, they felt the beating of his heart like the blows of a hammer, while at the same time they experienced great spiritual consolation.

This palpitation was accompanied by such a sensation of heat, that even at night, and in the coldest weather, he was obliged to open the windows of his room, and to use every other expedient to cool himself. He used to wear his habit unbuttoned down to the waist; and when his friends remonstrated with him in winter for being so imprudent, he would reply that he could not do otherwise, because he suffered so much from heat. One day, when he was an old man, he happened to be walking through Rome with some of his young penitents, and the snow falling thick around them, they could scarcely bear the cold, while he went along cheerfully with his habit open as usual; whereupon he began to laugh at them, saying, "Shame! shame! that young men should shrink from the cold while old men brave it." Pope Gregory XIII, having issued an order that confessors should wear their cottas in the confessional, Philip went to an audience of his Holiness with his habit unbuttoned; whereupon the Pope, expressing his surprise at his coming to him in such a costume, Philip replied, "I cannot even bear my habit buttoned, and your Holiness will have me wear a cotta in addition." "No, no," answered the Pope, "the order is intended for others and not for you;" and thus he gained a special exemption.

One of the most remarkable circumstances attending this palpitation was that it gave him no pain, and was under his own control. A short time before his death he said to Cardinal Frederic Borromeo, "Do not think that it gives me any pain, or has ever given me any; for I have always been as free from pain in connection with it as I am now. Moreover, I can check it whenever I wish; but when I am praying I never do so, because I do not choose to distract myself by thinking about it."

After having thus received the Holy Spirit in a visible form, Philip experienced a great increase of sensible devotion, and his fervour often rose to such a pitch, that, unable to endure the fire of love within him, he would throw himself down, and rolling on the ground, would exclaim, "No more, Lord, no more!" At length one day, when he was thus overcome, and had thrown himself on the ground, feeling as if he must expire, he cried out, "My God, I cannot bear so much; my Lord, I cannot bear it. Stop, Lord, or I shall die." His prayer was heard, and from that time his sensible devotion gradually diminished, so that when he came to be an old man he used to say: "When I was young I was more spiritual than I am now." It is not surprising that, being so filled with God, he would frequently say, "That to one who truly loves God, nothing is more irksome than life;" or that he would often repeat the words: "The true servants of God regard life with patience and desire death."

Philip always made light of this extraordinary gift, and, with his usual humility, did all he could to conceal it, speaking of the palpitation as a natural infirmity, or as a bad habit which he had picked up in his youth, and wearing his handkerchief over his heart in order to hide the tumour.

CHAPTER V

HE MIRACULOUS gift of the Holy Spirit made no change in Philip's outward life. He continued, as before, to spend the day in visiting the hospitals, instructing the poor, and exhorting sinners to repentance; and when evening drew on, he would retire to some solitary church or catacomb, where he would pass the night in prayer. The sort of life which he led, began to be observed; and Francesco Cardone, a Dominican, pointed him out to his novices as a saint, who had lived for ten years in the Catacomb of St. Calixtus, doing penance, and fasting on bread and herbs. The number of conversions which he effected, also attracted notice; and though only a layman, he was sought out by many who were in need of spiritual aid.

Philip originated at this time what has since grown into the great confraternity of the *Santissima Trinità*. Its original object was the performance of certain spiritual exercises and the frequentation of the sacraments. It was also the means of introducing into Rome, A.D. 1548, the devotion of the Quarant' Ore,[4] which had been first practised in Milan A.D. 1534.

The confraternity was established at the church of San Salvatore in Campo, on the 16th August, A.D. 1548, at Philip's suggestion, by his confessor, Father Persiano Rosa, one of the priests of St. Girolamo da Carla. Its commencement was very humble, for the original members, fifteen in number, were all of them poor and unknown, but persons of great piety. They were in the habit of meeting in

---

[4] Forty Hours. -Editor

the above church to receive the sacraments and perform their spiritual exercises, and on the first Sunday in every month the devotion of the *Quarant' Ore* was set up. On these occasions the brothers took it in turn to watch before the Blessed Sacrament, while Philip, to whom they looked up as to their father, gave instructions suited to the season, never quitting the church till the devotion closed, but remaining there day and night in the enjoyment of his Lord's presence. He used to keep by him a little bell, with which he would give the sign to the watchers to relieve each other; and as he dismissed those whose hour had just closed, he would seize the opportunity for exciting their zeal and fervour, often saying to them, "Away, now, brothers; your hour of prayer is finished, but not the time for doing good."

The year 1550 was that of the Jubilee, and the concourse of pilgrims to Rome being immense, the brothers ventured to hire a small house for the reception of some of the poorest; but this house proving too small for their purpose, they soon after removed to a larger one, which was lent them by a charitable person. Notwithstanding their moderate means, God so blessed their work that they were always prepared to meet the calls on their charity; and before the year expired their fame had so spread through Rome, that persons of all classes begged to join them. They were now able to purchase a suitable house, and thus a permanent character was given to the work which Philip had begun in such a humble way.

The object of the confraternity was also enlarged; for as their house remained vacant, except at those holy seasons when pilgrims flock to Rome, they determined to use it at other times as an hospital for convalescents.

In succeeding jubilees, the number of pilgrims who were received by the confraternity was proportionate to the increased number of its members, those in the jubilee of

A.D. 1600 amounting to 270,000. Cardinals, prelates, Roman nobles, ladies of the highest rank, and even the Pope himself, were then seen vying with each other in performing the most menial offices for the poor pilgrims. During this jubilee Clement VIII set an example which has been followed by his successors, often going to visit the pilgrims, washing their feet, blessing their meals, waiting on them at table, and performing other servile offices for them.

While Philip was thus pursuing his usual mode of life, his old longings after solitude returned with such force, that he had almost made up his mind to leave Rome and retire to some wild and desert spot, where he could spend the rest of his days in prayer; and he only waited to know with fuller certainty that this was what God required of him. Before very long the light which he sought was given him. He had been praying, as usual, through the livelong night, and just as day began to dawn, there stood before him a glorious form, in whom he recognized St. John the Baptist. Filled with joy and reverence, his heart palpitated with more than common violence, and his whole frame was agitated by a supernatural tremour, while St. John revealed to him that it was the will of God that he should remain in Rome, practising the greatest poverty and detachment, and continuing to serve Him by drawing souls into the way of salvation. The vision then vanished, leaving Philip with a sensible increase of fervour, which remained with him till his death.

On another occasion there appeared to him two souls clothed with glory, one of whom seemed to be eating a piece of dry bread; and on Philip's inquiring what this vision signified, a voice answered: "It is the will of God that thou shouldst live in the midst of Rome as if thou wert in a hermitage, abstaining, as far as thou canst, from eating meat." From this time Philip never ate meat, except when he was ill, or in condescension to the wishes of those around him; but when he was asked his reason for this abstinence, his humility led him to answer that meat did not agree with him.

CHAPTER VI

I N THE YEAR 1551, Philip's confessor, Father Persiano Rosa, proposed to him to take holy orders. At first he objected, on the ground of his unworthiness, and his great desire to serve God as a layman. Persiano Rosa, however, insisted; and Philip, who had long accustomed himself to bow his own judgment to that of his superiors, at last consented. In the month of March, A.D. 1561, he received the tonsure, the four minor orders, and the sub-diaconate in the church of St. Tommaso in Parione; on the following Holy Saturday he was ordained deacon at St. John Lateran; and on the 23rd of May of the same year he was ordained priest at St. Tommaso in Parione. In the course of the year he received faculties for hearing confessions.

As soon as Philip was ordained priest, he went to live at St. Girolamo da Carità. There happened to be then residing there his confessor, Persiano Rosa, and three other priests, all of them very holy men, who, though they did not live in common, and were bound by no rule, yet dwelt together in a happy union of fraternal love, joining together in prayer and the administration of the sacraments, and vying with each other how to reap a larger harvest of souls for God. This was a happy society for Philip to enter on his ordination, and he was no small acquisition to it.

Philip lost no time in commencing his new duties. The custom of saying Mass daily, had fallen into disuse at Rome till he revived it. He never failed, when he was in health, to say Mass every day, and he recommended the priests, who were his penitents, to do the same. He used to say that those who omitted their Mass for some trifling reason, such as giving themselves rest or recreation, erred greatly: "For," said he, "he who looks for recreation out of the Creator, and for consolation out of Christ, will never find them. He who seeks for consolation in any but the right place, seeks his own damnation; and he who wishes to be wise without the true wisdom, or to save himself without the Saviour, is not in health, but sick; he is not wise, but a fool." His fervour in celebrating Mass was so great, that while others found it necessary to prepare themselves by meditation, he was obliged to use every means to distract himself, fearing that otherwise the vehemence of his affections would throw him into an ecstasy, and he should not be able to begin the Mass, or when begun to finish it. While he was celebrating, the tears would roll down his cheeks, and he was often so overcome as to be forced to stand at the altar silent and motionless, waiting till he recovered the strength which the effusion of divine love had exhausted, while on other occasions he would be so abstracted that the server would have to pull his vestment in order to recall him. When he came to the Offertory, the joy which he experienced in merely touching the chalice, agitated him so greatly that he could scarcely pour out the wine and water, and he was generally obliged to steady his arm by leaning it on the altar. As the Mass proceeded, and the most solemn part of the adorable Sacrifice drew near, his joyousness visibly increased. All his movements were quick and rapid, yet there was nothing ungainly or abrupt in them; all was graceful and beautiful, so that the bystanders were moved to extraordinary devotion by the wonderful sight. His body seemed to be swayed by some invisible spirit, rather than by the ordinary laws of gravity. At the Memento, when he was praying for others, he trembled with supernatural emotion. At the Elevation, he would, at times, remain transfixed, with his arms raised in the air, so that he got into the habit of elevating the Host very slightly, and lowering it as quickly as he could. After the consecration, he seemed to be lifted up towards heaven, and often only just touched the ground with the extremities of his feet, so that, his inward joy appeared to find a vent in the undulatory movement of a sort of mystic dance of exultation, like that of David before the ark. When he took up the Body of our Lord in order to communicate himself, he became agitated in the same way as at the consecration, and in communicating he tasted an extraordinary sweetness. When he came to receive the chalice, no words can express his evident joy. It seemed as though he could not separate himself from the Precious Blood, and those who served his Mass were directed not to offer him the ablution till he should give them a sign to do so. When he had finished the Mass, and made his thanksgiving, he would retire to his room, pale and exhausted, and so abstracted that he did not recognize those whom he chanced to meet. He was so unwilling to have it supposed that there was anything unusual in his Mass, that if he celebrated at a side-altar, he would place himself so that no one could see his countenance, and he was careful always to be served by those who knew his ways, and would recall him when he became abstracted. For the same reason, he often said the last Mass when fewer persons would be in the church.

His extraordinary fervour procured for him many great favours. Once when he was saying Mass at the Torre de' Specchi, the nuns saw him raised three or four palms from the ground. A little girl also saw him at St. Girolamo raised two palms from the ground; whereupon turning to her mother, she said with great simplicity, "Mother, that Father must be possessed. Look how he stands up in the air." But her mother answered, "Hush! he is a saint, and he is in an ecstasy." One of his penitents, Sulpizia Sirleti, seeing him thus raised up, said to herself, "The Father must be possessed, for he is standing up in the air;" and going soon after to confession, and being about to mention this thought, she hesitated; but Philip pressing her to proceed, she began to say: "The other morning, when you were saying Mass, and were raised up in the air;" whereupon Philip putting his finger on his lips, exclaimed, "Hush, be silent." But she continued, "Then I said in my heart, 'The Father must be possessed.'" On hearing which, Philip smiled, and said repeatedly, "It is quite true, I am possessed. It is quite true, I am possessed."

A girl about twelve years old also saw him at St. Girolamo raised up in the air, and enveloped in a white and luminous cloud; and, though she knew that his vestment was red, it seemed to her to be white and sparkling. Muzio Achillei, one of the priests of San Severino, also saw his face resplendent like gold; and Aurelio Bacci, a native of Sienna, once saw him with a glory, about four fingers wide, round his head, which continued there till he had communicated. One day Cesare Tomasi, one of his penitents, observed that he had made a long pause at the consecration, just after having replaced the Host upon the altar; and when he had returned to the sacristy after the Mass, Tomasi asked him why he had done so. But Philip, smiling, put his hand on Tomasi's head, and was silent; whereupon Tomasi pressed him more earnestly to tell him the reason of the pause; till at last the saint, overcome by his entreaties, answered, that sometimes during his Mass, God did him the favour to show him the glories of Paradise.

As for the favours and graces which he obtained for others by his Mass, such as recovering them from dangerous illness, or curing them of bad habits, or filling them with compunction, and sometimes converting them to the faith, it would far outstrip our limits to recount even a small portion of them.

Philip's zeal in administering the sacrament of penance, was not inferior to his fervour in offering up the Holy Sacrifice. At that time the sacraments were so neglected, that few persons went to confession and communion more than once a year, and many not even so often. Philip, therefore, made it one of his great objects to rouse them from this cold indifference, and draw them on to the constant use of the sacraments, and especially to that of penance. At the first peep of day, as soon as the church was open, he would go down to his confessional, and there he would remain the whole morning, never quitting his post unless some duty forced him to do so. If no one came to him he would read, or say his office, or repeat the Rosary, and sometimes he would go into the street, and walk up and down before the door, hoping thus to catch those who were passing by, and who might be entering the church. Even after he had left the church he was equally ready to hear confessions, his room being open to men at all hours, whether of the day or night; and he was so anxious that his penitents should have free access to him at all times, that when he went to rest, he would put the key of his room under the door, so that they might come in even if he were in bed. He had such a thirst for the salvation of souls, that it gave him the greatest pleasure even to sit in the confessional; and he used to say that God granted him special spiritual consolations, in order to enable him to support the bodily fatigue which he underwent in the performance of his duties as a confessor. Even when he was ill he could not be induced to give up hearing confessions, unless the physicians ordered him to do so; and if people remonstrated with him for thus fatiguing himself; he would answer, that it was not a fatigue, but only rest and recreation to him.

Philip's zeal for souls was not, however, limited to the administration of the sacraments. Not content with having sown the good seed, he spared no pains to encourage its growth, and bring its fruit to perfection. In the afternoon, when he left the church, and retired to his own room, he would ask two or three of his penitents to accompany him, gradually extending the invitation to all who could be induced to come; and there, while they stood in a circle around him, he would sometimes talk to them about the contempt of the world, or the beauty of virtue, or the love of God, or some other subject calculated to excite their devotion; and at other times he would set them to read the life of a saint, or would start some subject on which, after each had given his opinion, he would discourse with his usual fervour. As he proceeded, he would become so exhausted by his affections, that he would throw himself on his bed, which would be shaken by the violence of his supernatural palpitation; while sometimes even the room would vibrate, and not unfrequently he would be so rapt in ecstasy, that he would be raised a hand's breadth above the bed, and would remain thus suspended in the air. Sometimes feeling as one held captive by Divine love, he would break forth with the lines:—

> "Vorrei saper da voi com' ella è fatta
> "Questa rete d' amor, che tanti ha preso."[5]

At other times he would exclaim: "Vulneratus charitate sum ego;"[6] and then, overcome by his interior emotions, he

---

[5] I would like to know from you how this net of love,
   So became that it caught so many men.
   -Editor.

[6] "I have been wounded by charity." - Editor.

would seem to languish with love, so that those who beheld him, could not but apply to him the words of the Spouse in the Canticle: "*Fulcite me floribus, stipate me malis, quia amore langueo.*"[7]

Such, then, was the way in which Philip spent the first years of his priesthood. His life may be summed up in the brief statement that he said Mass daily, that he was assiduous in his attendance in the confessional, and that he spent his leisure hours in conversing with his friends on spiritual subjects, a humble and simple mode of life, and remarkable only for the way in which it was united with the most wonderful supernatural gifts.

---

[7] "Support me with flowers, surround me with apples, because I languish with love." -Editor.

San Girolamo della Carità
Where St. Philip began his mission

San Girolamo della Carità
Side altar where St. Philip Neri said his Masses
The inventive altar rail was made in the 17th century by Antonio
Giorgetti, a pupil of Bernini

CHAPTER VII

ut though Philip's conduct was so simple, it suffced to draw down persecution. Among the deputies of the Church of St. Girolamo there happened to be a physician; Vincenzio Teccosi, who, feeling that Philip's holiness was a tacit reproach on his own worldliness, took a great dislike to him, and became very anxious to get rid of him. It also happened that two of the sacristans were apostate monks, who, though no one suspected it, had broken their vows and left their convent; and as Philip's virtue was to them like coals of fire poured on their consciences, they gladly conspired with Vincenzio Teccosi to drive him from the church. They accordingly began by scoffing at his devotion, turning his fervour into ridicule, and laughing at his saintly peculiarities. Finding, however, that this had no effect, but that he seemed pleased to be treated with contempt, and was ever ready to join the laugh against himself, they proceeded to greater lengths. When he came to prepare for saying Mass, they would shut the door of the sacristy in his face, and forbid him to enter; and when at length they admitted him, they would sometimes refuse to let him have the vestments, or would give him only torn and dirty ones; and at other times they would snatch the missal or the chalice out of his hands, or they would hide first one thing and then another, obliging him to make a vexatious search before he could procure what was necessary. Sometimes when he was vested they would force him to unrobe, or if he went to one altar they would insult him publicly by driving him to another, or making him return to the sacristy, loading him at all times with the coarsest abuse, to which they not unfrequently added blows.

Philip, however, was not the least disturbed by their conduct. He received their insults with perfect sweetness and humility; he uttered no word of complaint or reproach, but always spoke well of his persecutors, and took every opportunity to serve them. His friends urged him to leave the place where he met with such unworthy treatment; but he would not entertain the thought of doing so, saying, that he would on no account fly from the cross which our Lord had laid on him. On one occasion, when the sacristans had been pushing him about very roughly, he said to Marcello Ferro, one of his penitents, who was standing by: "See how they treat me; but let us pray to God for them." The more, however, he tried to conciliate them, the more violent they became. Kind words, gentle expostulations, serious admonitions, all were in vain; their animosity only increased from day to day, for perceiving that he was not insensible to their conduct, they began to hope that they should soon drive him away. In this, however, they were quite mistaken, for the only effect which these annoyances had on Philip was to make him redouble his prayers for patience. At last, one morning, above two years after the commencement of the persecution, as he was saying Mass, he fixed his eyes on the crucifix, and broke into the gentle expostulation: "Oh! good Jesus, why wilt Thou not listen to me? I have been asking Thee so long and so earnestly for patience, and Thou hast not yet granted my prayer." Then he heard within him a voice which said to him: "Wast thou not asking for patience? Know then that before long I will give it thee, but on condition that if thou sincerely desire it thou shalt gain it by means of these trials." Cheered by these words, Philip felt his courage revive, and resting his confidence in the Divine aid, he joyfully resigned himself to bear his persecutions so long as it should be the will of God that they should continue. He had not, however, long to wait for his reward. One day, soon after, as he was going through a passage which led to the sacristy, one of the sacristans loaded him with such vile abuse, that his comrade, touched at the sight of Philip's extraordinary patience, rose suddenly in his defence, and rushing upon his late associate, seized him by the throat, and would have strangled him if Philip had not come to his rescue. Then, remembering that he himself was no less guilty, he threw himself at Philip's feet, begging his pardon and his prayers, and confessing not only his offences against himself, but his more grievous sin in breaking his vows. From this time he conceived a great affection for Philip, proclaiming him everywhere to be a saint; and before very long, with the help of Philip's prayers and admonitions, he was perfectly converted, and returned to his convent.

Vincenzo Teccosi soon followed this good example, and in the presence of several persons, threw himself at Philip's feet and begged his pardon. He afterwards placed himself entirely under Philip's direction, and became one of his most attached and obedient penitents, never allowing a day to pass without going to see him.

When the devil found himself foiled in this attack on Philip's patience, he tried what he could do to alarm and disturb him. With this view he would often appear to him when he was praying at night; but Philip took no notice of him, but invoking Our Lady's aid, went on praying as usual. One day, too, as he was passing the Baths of Diocletian, he saw, as he thought, a young man sitting on a wall; but on looking more closely and steadily at him, he perceived that his face was constantly changing, so that at one moment he looked young, and at the next, old. This convinced him that the being before him was no other than the spirit of evil; and so fortifying himself with the sign of the cross, he went boldly up to him and commanded him to depart, whereupon the devil instantly disappeared.

The Baths of Diocletian
Present day site of the Church of Santa Maria degli Angeli e Martyri, built on the site by Michaelangelo Buonarotti

St. Philip Neri in Ecstasy
Guercino, 1656

CHAPTER VIII

T WAS little wonder that the devil should persecute Philip, for he was now reaping such a harvest of souls, that the powers of hell trembled at his very name. Six years had elapsed since his ordination, and during all this time he had continued to lead the simple, unostentatious life that has been already described. Morning after morning he had taken his post at dawn by his confessional, patiently waiting in the church for the repentant prodigal, or pacing before the door to catch the thoughtless wanderer; day after day he had offered up the Holy Sacrifice for the conversion of sinners; and each recurring afternoon he was to be seen in his little room, lavishing his strength, his affections, his natural talents, and his supernatural gifts on all whom he could hope to lure to the Fountain of Living Water. It was weary work, too commonplace, and at first scarcely fruitful enough to satisfy the cravings of a soul burning with an apostle's zeal and a martyr's love; nay, it might be a question whether so ordinary a life was an adequate compensation for the sacrifice of solitude which it cost. Still, however, Philip persevered; and as years rolled on, the fruit began to appear. He had not now to wait in loitering expectation by his confessional, for his penitents increased from day to day, and as years passed on they became so numerous, that as many as forty would sometimes come to him before daybreak, and it was noon before he had done with them.

At first he had been followed to his room by only two or three of his spiritual children; but now the crowd was so great that the little chamber would not contain them all. His first converts had been picked up in shops, and banks, and among the poor in public thoroughfares; but now the rich, the learned and the noble, priests and laymen, prelates and cardinals, began to gather round him. His bright eye, his gentle voice, the easy flow of his conversation, and above all, his sweet, loving manner, at first attracted them; but when they were once drawn within his magic circle, there was a strange fascination about him which they could not resist, and which drew them on insensibly into the atmosphere of purity and love in which he himself dwelt. And then the sinner would be forced to hate his sin, and the worldly man would be disgusted with riches and honours, and he who had hitherto lived only for self, would turn his eyes to contemplate the self-denying love of a dying Saviour; till at last, one after another, they would feel themselves constrained to break through the shackles that bound their souls, and falling at Philip's feet, would confess their past sins, and ask him to guide their future steps.

Nor were these conversions mere passing impulses, which might be accounted for by the ordinary influence of a superior mind like Philip's. For, on the contrary, time only strengthened the resolutions which had been made at the first awakening of compunction; and as Divine love penetrated deeper and deeper into the hearts of Philip's converts, they offered themselves so freely and so joyfully to God, that there seemed to be no limit to their fervour and perseverance. Thus by the time that Philip had been six years a priest, there was gathered round him a band of noble and heroic spirits, well worthy to be called the sons of such a father.

There was the young Cæsar Baronius, whom his parents had sent to Rome to study law, making sure that his great talents would raise him to the highest honours. But he fell in with Philip, and he was soon inspired with such fervour that he became the talk of the town; and though he did not neglect his studies, his parents took the alarm, and threatened to cast him off if he did not give up his devotional practices. But the threat had no effect; he preferred God to wealth and dignities; and having made his choice, he was thrown penniless on the world, and henceforth placed himself in Philip's hands, binding himself to him by a vow of obedience.

Then there was Giovan Battista Salviati, brother to Cardinal Salviati, and cousin to Catherine de' Medici, queen of France, a man devoted to worldly vanities; but being persuaded by his wife, Porzia de' Massimi, to make Philip's acquaintance, he imbibed such a spirit of love and humility, that he spent his whole time in active works of charity, and was induced only by Philip's command to retain the dress and retinue befitting his rank

Besides these, there was Francesco Maria Tarugi, the relative of Popes Julius and Marcellus, a man no less distinguished by his talents than his birth. He came to confess to Philip on the occasion of a jubilee; and Philip took him to his room, and praying with him for an hour, inspired him with such devotion and sweetness, that though Tarugi had never before practised mental prayer, the hour seemed to be only a few minutes. He returned again and again to St. Girolamo, and at last conceived a great desire to give himself to God. There were, however, some obstacles, but Philip assured him they would soon be removed; and before a month had elapsed, Philip's words proved true. Tarugi now made a general confession, and as he proceeded, Philip took the words out of his month, and revealed to him his most secret thoughts and most hidden sins; and from this time Tarugi renounced his worldly prospects, and gave himself so entirely into Philip's hands, that when he came to be an archbishop and a cardinal, his proudest boast was, that for fifty years he had been Philip's novice.

It was whispered, too, among Philip's penitents, that he could see into the future. In 1556, Guglielmo Bucca being ill, Philip foretold that he would die, and so it came to pass. The husband of Fulgeria Ancrea objected to her frequenting the sacraments, saying, that he did not wish to have so much devotion in his family; but Philip bade her persevere, assuring her that her husband would soon follow her example; and within a very short time he placed himself under Philip's direction, and continued to obey him till his dying day. One day, Philip fell in with a Jew in the church of St. John Lateran, and said to him: "My good fellow, listen to me and repeat after me the following words, 'If thou Christ art the true God, inspire me with faith to believe in thee.'" But the Jew refused, because that prayer would imply a doubt in his own creed. Then Philip, turning to the bystanders, exhorted them to pray for the poor unbeliever, "for," added he, "he will soon be a Christian;" and before many days had elapsed, the Jew was converted and baptized.

Philip's prayers, too, were found to have peculiar power with God. In the year 1549, while he was still a layman, he had been sought out by Prospero Crivelli, cashier in one of the principal banks of Rome, who had been refused absolution by a Jesuit Father. In great trouble, he went to Philip, who soon discovered that, though his heart was touched with compunction, he had not resolution to break away from confirmed habits of sin. He therefore said to him all that was calculated to strengthen his feeble resolutions for good, and finally dismissed him, saying: "Go, I will pray for you, and I will pray so earnestly that you will relinquish these sins." And so it came to pass; for Prospero soon after reformed his life, and henceforth gave himself up entirely to Philip's guidance. In 1554, Prospero was so ill that the priest had been sent for to recommend his soul, when Philip came to see him and said: "I will go at once to St. Peter's, and pray our Lord that you may not die; and if I cannot save your life in any other way, I will offer my life for yours, begging that your disease may come on me, and that you may be restored to health." While Philip prayed at St. Peter's, Prospero fell asleep, and at the end of a quarter of an hour he awoke perfectly cured.

Giovan Battista Modio, an author of some note in his day, and one of Philip's earliest penitents, was so dangerously ill, that his friends expected each moment to be his last. Philip came to see him, and retiring to an adjoining room to pray for him, he was seen, as he prayed, to be raised some feet from the floor, and to be surrounded with a resplendent light. At length he came to himself, and returned to the room of the dying man; when, placing his hand on his head, he cried out: "Giovan Battista, you will not die this time; you will soon be well." At these words, Modio recovered his speech, and began to talk to Philip as if he were quite well; and from this time he continued to amend so rapidly, that in a few days he was able to resume his usual occupations.

While Philip was thus diffusing spiritual light and warmth around him, the fire of divine love was ever burning more and more brightly within his own bosom, so that it was no easy task for him to confine within the limits of his humble sphere the loving ardour which consumed him. A few years before, the Jesuit Fathers had set out for the East, and their letters were now arriving in Rome. These letters were taken to Philip's room, and the glorious accounts of St. Francis Xavier's success were read over and over with breathless interest. It was Philip's lifelong complaint, that he had never done or suffered anything for Jesus; and now that others were toiling amid savage tribes and under scorching suns, and the martyr's crown was suspended over their heads, he sighed to think that he was dwelling at ease in a city of palaces. He had long hoped and prayed for such a time as this, and now that the prize was within his sight, he must follow on and seize it. He confided his thoughts to his most intimate friends, twenty of whom, including Francesco Maria Tarugi and Giovan Battista Modio, shared his feelings and offered to accompany him. They prayed long and fervently, and as time passed on, their resolution became the stronger, till at length Philip determined, as a final step, to seek from others the confirmation of his own opinion.

There happened at this time to be in Rome a Cistercian monk, Agostino Ghettini, prior of the convent of SS. Vincent and Anastasius, at the Tre Fontane, who had a high reputation for sanctity. To him Philip went, and opening his mind to him, begged him to inquire what was the will of God. The monk undertook to do so, and bade Philip return in a few days for his answer. On the appointed day Philip and his companions repaired to the Tre Fontane. Hope was high in their hearts, and it was a hope that could not be disappointed; for though they panted to take up the missioner's cross, and to set out in search of suffering and of death, yet there was within them a calm and loving confidence, which whispered to them that even the martyr's crown is less bright and precious than the sweet and holy will of God. There are few places more calculated to stir up the love of souls and the desire for martyrdom than the Tre Fontane;[8] and as the devoted band knelt over the spot where the Apostle had shed his blood, they could not but unite themselves with the joy that had thrilled through his soul when his severed head thrice leaped exultingly, and the one

---

[8] S. Paul was beheaded at the Tre Fontane, and tradition tells that when his head was cut off, it gave three successive leaps, and at each leap, the name of Jesus burst from his lips, while on each spot on which the head rested there gushed forth a fountain of water.

loved Name burst from his quivering lips. The monk soon joined them, and then a few words sealed their fate. He told them that St. John the Evangelist had appeared to him, and had revealed to him that Rome was to be Philip's Indies, and that our Lord would make use of him and his disciples for the salvation of many. They knelt once more in prayer and thanksgiving, and then they turned their steps homewards, wending their way back to the city with far different thoughts from those which had filled their minds when they had trodden the same road a few hours before. Still, no secret disappointment mingled with the peace and joy which reigned in their hearts, for their only wish had been to know and do the will of God; and though the words they had heard were strange and mysterious, they felt assured that God would guide them in their unlooked for missionary career.

CHAPTER IX

hilip had now received his mission, and from this time forth, though we still hear of his yearnings for a hermit's solitude, and for the martyr's crown, yet during the remaining forty years of his life, his heart was cheerfully fixed on the task which our Lord had assigned him, and in which he found the most ample scope for his missionary zeal.

In considering the means which Philip adopted to carry out his mission, two things at once strike us. The first is, their exceeding simplicity. His sole arms are the Sacraments of the Church, and the practices which she recommends to her children. His motive is obvious. For as his work lay not with any peculiar class, but with persons of every rank and station, he had need of some universal medicine, and he could not hope to find such except in the treasury of that Church, the essence of whose ordinances is their Catholicity.

The other point is that he seems always to have had in his mind the idea of the primitive Church. During those long vigils in the catacombs, among the tombs of martyrs, and virgins, and saints of every grade, he had been carried into the bosom of the early Church, and had learnt how it was that she had triumphed. She lived in the midst of her enemies, the Christian wife united to a Pagan husband, the virgin spouse of Christ dwelling under the roof of profligate parents, the Christian slave crushed under the yoke of a brutal Pagan master, and a man's bitterest foes too often those of his own family and household. And yet, in spite of this close contact with blasphemy and the foulest impurity, never had her faith been brighter, nor her purity more spotless. She seemed to live by miracle, and yet in truth she lived only by simple faith, and the ordinances of her Lord. Each day, before the morning dawned, her children assembled in the subterranean sanctuary, to fortify their souls by prayer and the word of God, and to be fed with the life-giving Body of the Lord before they sallied forth to meet their several trials; and on each returning eve they met again, to be refreshed by prayer and the word of God. They gave their wealth to the Church and to the poor; they devoted their time and strength to the service of the sick and helpless; and thus knit together in charity, and loosed from every worldly tie, they stood prepared to resist the world's malice and the persecutor's fury. But, lest they should be tempted unawares to cling to some earthly treasure, the Church would summon them, on each recurring martyr's festival, to meet around the martyr's grave, and there, while the Holy Sacrifice was being offered in his honour, they would in spirit lay themselves upon the altar and offer themselves up as living sacrifices, not knowing whether, before the day should close, they might not be called, like him whose memory they celebrated, to shed their blood for Jesus. Their only weapons in this deadly combat had been the Sacraments, prayer, the word of God, mutual charity, and perfect detachment; and Philip had, therefore, no hesitation in trusting to these alone for the conversion of Rome.

When Philip set about his task, he found that he had been unconsciously laying the foundation for it, and that he had now only to give a definite and formal character to what he had already begun. The afternoon meetings in his little chamber were now so well attended, that the room would not hold all who came, and some new arrangement was unavoidable. He therefore applied to the deputies of the Church of St. Girolamo, and obtained from them permission to build an oratory over one of the naves of the church. As soon as it was completed he transferred the afternoon meetings to it, A.D. 1558, and at the same time he instituted the spiritual exercises, which were the seed of the future oratory.

The meetings in the oratory took place twice every day, in the afternoon and in the evening. The afternoon meeting opened with prayer and the singing of a hymn, after which one of those who were present read some spiritual book, Philip sometimes interrupting the reader with observations calculated to explain or enforce what was read, and at others, calling on some of the others to give their opinion on it. The reading lasted half an hour, and was succeeded by three short sermons of half an hour each, delivered in the simplest style, without any pretence at learning or verbal ornament; and after the sermons, prayer and singing of hymns closed the meeting.

The first preachers in the oratory were Tarugi and Giovanni Battista Modio, both of them laymen; Baronius, Bordino, and Antonio Fucci, were soon after associated with them; and as time went on, others were added. Philip forbade them to touch on questions of theology, saying, that those who wish to be learned in such matters, could go to the schools; but he bade them confine themselves to subjects which would be generally useful, inciting men to love virtue and hate sin, to despise the world, to love suffering and mortification, and to set their affections on the joys of Paradise and union with God. He particularly urged them to enforce all their instructions by the examples of the saints, as he himself never failed to do; and with the same view he appointed Giovanni Battista Modio, and after his death, Antonio Fucci, to narrate the lives of the saints; and a few years later, he set Baronius the task of relating the history of the Church from the birth of our Lord up to that time. He made such a point of encouraging humility both in the preacher and his hearers, that if any of his sons overstepped the bounds which he had imposed on them, he would instantly check them, and, desiring them to sit down, would take their place, correct their errors, and set forth the subject in his own simple and humble way.

The evening meetings had prayer and penance for their exclusive object. They opened with half an hour's mental prayer, which was succeeded by a selection of vocal prayers, varying on different days of the week, but all of them such as are in common use in the Church on Mondays, Wednesdays, and Fridays, which were the days appointed for the penitential exercise. At the conclusion of the mental prayer, the door of the oratory was closed, and the windows were darkened, so that nothing was visible except a small crucifix, on which the light was thrown from a dark lantern; and then, after the chief points of the Passion had been read aloud, all who were present used the discipline while they recited in a low voice the *Miserere* and *De Profundis*. Then followed a certain number of *Paters* and *Aves* for perseverance in God's service, for the souls in Purgatory, for the wants of the Church, and the intentions of the members of the Oratory; after which the *Nunc Dimittis* and some collects were said, the whole closing with the Antiphon of our Lady, according to the season of the year. On Tuesdays and Thursdays, the Litany of the Saints succeeded the mental prayer, and was followed by the Paters and Aves, and by the Antiphon of our Lady as above; while on Saturdays and Feasts of our Lady, the Litany of Loretto took the place of the Litany of the Saints.

The leading features of this simple form of devotion will at once be seen to be a preference for the Church's ordinary devotions, faith in the prayers of our Lady and the saints, and deep contrition for sin, in union with the passion of a crucified Saviour; while the use of the discipline in a mixed assembly of men, living in the world, may be considered as laying down the broad principle that corporal penances are not ascetic practices peculiar to the cloister and the desert.

CHAPTER X

HE NEXT POINT to which Philip turned his attention, was the training of his penitents to active works of charity. He had always been in the habit of visiting the hospitals, which were then little more than receptacles for the sick, who were left dependant on their friends, or the casual charity of strangers, for the supply of all their wants. In primitive times, and indeed long since, it had been the custom for charitable persons to visit the hospitals and minister to the wants of the sick; but this pious practice had long fallen into disuse, till Philip revived it. He had from an early period been accompanied in his visits, by a few intimate friends; but now such numbers were found willing to join him that it was necessary to adopt some more regular system. It, therefore, became his custom to assemble them in the morning at St. Girolamo, when, after they had made their confessions and heard Mass, and received holy Communion, he would divide them into three little bands, and send them forth in silence and recollection to visit the Hospitals of St. John Lateran, our Lady of Consolation, and the Santo Spirito, he himself generally accompanying one or other of the parties. Every morning there would be from thirty to forty visitors, and on festivals a much larger number; for on these last such of his penitents as lived by their own labour, were disengaged, and joyfully devoted their holiday to this work of love.

Few occupations afford better opportunities for the exercise of true charity, and its inseparable companion, mortification, than attendance on the sick poor; for without aiming at any of those heroic acts by which saints have conquered their natural repugnances, the common charitable works of dressing the wounds of the poor, washing their neglected persons, making their beds, and cleaning their rooms, are naturally most repulsive. And yet it was to these that Philip trained the proud and voluptuous Romans, who had been nursed in the lap of luxury, and had hitherto spent their lives in the pursuit of pleasure, and the enjoyment of literature, the fine arts, and all those refinements which the world employs to captivate the senses and enslave the souls of its votaries. In order to encourage them to persevere in a work which must have been most trying to them, he would tell them that once, about A.D. 1550, a person, apparently in the most destitute condition, had asked him for charity, when, being touched with the deepest compassion, he had instantly offered the beggar the few pence which constituted the whole of his worldly wealth; whereupon the beggar, who was none other than an angel, replied: "I wished to see what you would do," and disappeared. He would also tell them that on one occasion, when two Fathers of the Order of Ministers of the Sick, established by his penitent, St. Camillus of Lellis, were recommending the souls of some dying persons, he had seen the angels standing by them and suggesting to them the words which they spoke.

But Philip's own example was the best encouragement which he could afford his penitents. One has often read beautiful stories of persons, who, on going to the bedside of some most disgusting object of charity, have found in the bed, not the loathsome invalid, but our dear Lord Himself; and so it ever was to Philip; for to him every object of charity was our Lord, and called out his deepest sympathies. He was never weary of waiting on the sick, ministering to their bodily wants with patient tenderness; procuring for them the little comforts which would soothe their sufferings, cheering them with words of spiritual consolation, and if they were dying, bringing them the Sacraments, helping them with his prayers, and never quitting them by day or night till he had seen them safely through their last great struggle. It was impossible to be with him, and not to catch his spirit; for he was ever so ready to perform the most loathsome or most menial office, that when he called on any of his penitents to do the like, his command, so far from being a hard obedience, seemed rather to be the generous transfer to them of a sweet task of love, or the gift of a bright jewel wherewith to enrich their heavenly crown. Thus he instilled into them such a noble, self-denying spirit, that nothing seemed too much to ask from them.

One day, in the year 1554, as Philip and his little band were going to the Hospital del Salvatore, they found a poor sick man lying in the street; whereupon Philip made a sign to one of his penitents, called Francesco, to carry the poor fellow to the hospital; and Francesco, without saying a word, took up the dying man, and putting him on his shoulders, carried him through the public street in broad daylight, without ever stopping till they reached the hospital.

On another occasion, Giovanni Battista Salviati found in one of the hospitals a man who had formerly been his servant, whereupon he told him to get up and let him make his bed. But the poor man, who had known Giovanni Battista only in his days of pride and worldliness, and was not aware what a change had since come over him, thought that he must be making sport of him, and feeling hurt at the ill-timed joke, he replied: "Ah! Signor Battista, this is not a time to make sport of a poor servant. Pray let me alone." It was in vain that Giovanni Battista assured him that he was not joking, the poor man would not believe him; and the more Giovanni Battista insisted, the more obstinate the other became in refusing to obey. At length, however, Giovanni Battista's charity and humility overcame the incredulity of his old servant, who being at last induced to get up, could scarcely believe the evidence of his own senses, when he saw himself waited on by the master in whose train he had formerly walked. Philip's charity, however, was not limited to visiting the sick in the hospitals, but included in its wide embrace all classes of persons and all kinds of distress, so that he never heard of a case of distress without making some effort to relieve it. If he was told of persons who were in want, he would go at once to visit them, sometimes carrying food to them concealed under his habit, and at other times recommending them to the charity of his more wealthy penitents. He had an especial compassion for those who were in a more respectable position in society, and who would, therefore, be ashamed to expose their necessities; and to such he would often carry relief at night, lest their feelings should be hurt by its becoming known to their neighbours that they had received an alms. Once he happened to be told that a poor lady could not go out for want of a gown, whereupon he instantly took off his habit and sent it to her. During a famine which took place in the year 1551, one of his friends having sent him six loaves, he at once gave them to a Spanish priest, who lived at St. Girolamo, and contented himself for that day with thirty olives, saying, that the Spaniard, being a foreigner, was not likely to be as well provided for as himself, who was well known in Rome.

He always kept behind his door a list of religious houses to which he was in the habit of sending alms. Several times a week he gave alms to persons who were in prison, frequently sending his penitents to visit them, and going himself to the Pope to intercede for those who were unjustly or cruelly imprisoned. He took great interest in orphans, and especially in poor girls, for numbers of whom he provided, either by putting them into convents, or by giving them dowers to enable them to marry respectably. He was also very compassionate towards those who lived by their labour, and had accidentally been unsuccessful. A poor chicory seller, having come one evening to the oratory, and being detained by violent rain, was in great trouble at having lost the sale of his chicory, on which he depended for his evening meal; but Philip, hearing his lamentations, bought a part of the chicory himself, and persuaded those who were with him to purchase the rest. At another time, happening to fall in with two brothers who had been watchmakers, but who had lost their customers in their old age and were then in great distress, he ordered them to make several watches, which he persuaded his more wealthy visitors to take off their hands.

Philip's tenderness of heart was not confined to all classes of human beings, but extended to all God's creatures. He could not bear that any living thing, however insignificant, should be made to suffer. One of the Fathers having carelessly trod on a lizard, he exclaimed with great indignation: "Cruel fellow! What harm has that poor worm done you?" And on another occasion, when he saw a butcher wantonly wound a poor dog with his knife, he was so distressed that he could not recover his composure for a considerable time. If birds, or other living animals, were sent to him, he would not allow them to be killed, but either set them at liberty, or entrusted them to some of his penitents to take care of.

There seemed, indeed, to be a sort of sympathy between him and the animal creation, somewhat akin to that strange power which the seraphic St. Francis exercised over it. Dogs easily attached themselves to him; even wild animals allowed him to caress them; while the following is a curious instance of the fearlessness with which he was regarded by little birds. One of his penitents, Louis Ames, having offered him two birds which sang beautifully, he accepted them on condition that Louis would come every day to feed them. One day, when Philip was ill, Louis came as usual to look after them, when, to his great surprise, he saw that they had left their cage, and that one was perched on Philip's face, while the other fluttered round him, singing most sweetly. Louis tried to drive them away, but in vain; for, so far from being frightened, they constantly returned to their old position; till at last Philip bade Louis bring the cage, and hold it open before them; and then, as if they had understood his command they instantly obeyed him, and flying into the cage, allowed themselves to be once more shut up in it.

CHAPTER XI

 UT it was not to active works of charity, nor to the daily word of God, nor even to prayer that Philip looked principally for the conversion of Rome. His chief dependance was placed on the sacraments, in which the soul of the sinner is washed from sin, and the pardoned prodigal receives the life-giving Body of his Lord. The Passion was the subject of his constant meditation, and so great was his devotion to it, that, in order to relieve the emotions which were excited by the thought of the sufferings of Jesus Crucified, he used to keep by him a crucifix which he had taken off the cross, and which he pressed from time to time to his heart, while, with tears and sighs, he gave vent to his grief in the touching lament of the martyr St. Ignatius: *"Amor meus crucifixus est. Amor meus crucifixus est."* His hatred for sin was in proportion to his devotion to the Passion; for, when he thought of sin, he saw in it that which had wrung the bloody sweat from the agonizing heart of Jesus, which had torn his sacred flesh with scourges, pierced his brow with thorns, watered the streets of Jerusalem with his blood, and so cruelly nailed Him to the cross. It was intolerable to him that the pure and spotless Body of his Lord should have been thus torn and wounded in vain, or that his Precious Blood should be set at nought by those for whom that Fountain of Love had been poured out; and hence his passionate longing to shed his own blood for Jesus; and when that was denied him, hence his burning thirst for the salvation of sinners. His desire for the conversion of sinners was so intense, that it seemed as

if it must be satisfied at any cost; and thus, when a soul resisted his ordinary efforts to convert it, or when a dying man was assailed by dangerous temptations, he would become so united with the love of God for sinners, that he would gladly have given his own life for the poor sinner before him, and he would pray so earnestly that the tears would gush from his eyes, his whole frame would tremble, and not unfrequently he would fall into an ecstasy.

The love of souls manifests itself in the saints in different ways, according to their several characters and vocations; in Philip it seemed to be peculiarly supernatural, and to partake simply of the character of that Spirit, whose fruits are patience, benignity, goodness, longanimity and mildness. Not only was his room open to all at all times, but if from respect or timidity, any one hesitated to enter, he would go to meet him, and, taking him by the hand, would draw him gently in. He would not allow persons to be sent away because he was busy, or was resting himself; and if he had reason to suspect that the other fathers intercepted those who were coming to him, he would go to their rooms, and if he found there any one desirous of speaking to him, he would reprove the father sharply, saying: "Have I not told you that I will not have any time or any hour to be my own?" He accommodated his manners to suit all who approached him, whether they were rich or poor, nobles or plebeians, young or old, learned or ignorant. When those whom he had never seen before came to visit him, he received them with the same joy and affection as if they had been old friends whom he had been long expecting; he lavished on all the same caresses and the same welcome, taking the same pains to help all, whether rich or poor, to the utmost extent of his power; and thus he so captivated all who approached him, that they could not but return again and again to see him, many continuing for thirty or forty years to visit him once or twice every day.

It has been already told how patiently he would sit by his confessional through the livelong morning, and how joyfully he would receive, whether by day or night, those who came to his room for confession. He seemed like some vendor of goods who was never weary of crying to the passers by: "All you that thirst, come to the waters . . . Make haste, buy and eat;" and provided he could find a purchaser for the Living Water which he was offering to all without money and without price, he cared not what fatigue it cost himself. He would often go out at night, in the cold, and wind, and rain, exposing himself to all weathers, and often even to danger, if there was the least hope of saving a soul; and, when one of his penitents one day said to him: "Father, you make yourself too cheap," he replied warmly: "I tell you that those of my penitents who are the most devout, are those whom I gained for our Lord by exposing myself at night to convert them; and be assured that nothing brings such consolation and sweetness to souls that love God, as leaving Christ for Christ."

And when he had succeeded in drawing sinners to the sacraments, he showed no less anxiety to retain them, condescending to their weakness, and carefully avoiding any severity which might drive them away. He would not have confessors make the path of virtue too difficult, especially to recent converts; and he admonished them not to be severe in the confessional, nor to reprove their penitents harshly, lest they should drive them to despair, but to compassionate them, and to speak gently and affectionately to them, condescending to them as much as possible, in order thereby to gain them the better. One of his penitents having committed a mortal sin, came to confess it; but shame overcame him, and he became so confused and distressed that he could not speak; whereupon Philip asked him kindly why he did not proceed with his confession, and the trembling sinner replied: "Because I am ashamed to mention a sin which I have committed." Then Philip, like a tender father pitying the misery of his erring child, took him by the hand and said in his own loving way: "Do not be afraid; I will tell you your sin." And forthwith he related the sin, with all its full particulars.

Another of his penitents was so enslaved by a certain sin, that he fell into it almost daily; but Philip, instead of reproving him, or imposing a severe penance, only bade him come and confess the sin each time he committed it, without waiting to fall into it a second time. The penitent obeyed; and each time, after confessing his sin, he was sent away with the same injunction; till at last, after this had gone on for several months, he found himself freed, not only from this sin, but from others to which he was addicted.

He was not in the habit of exclaiming against the love of dress and similar vanities, especially in women, saying, that one must put up for a time with such imperfections in beginners, for that they will lay them by of their own accord as soon as they have acquired some devotion. Thus, a lady who wore the high-heeled shoes which were then the height of the fashion, asked him if it was wrong to do so; but he only answered: "Take care you do not fall." Also to a young man who wore a more than usually large ruff, he said: "I would caress you more frequently if your ruff did not hurt my hands." Before very long, however, both the high heels and the ruff were laid aside.

But the great secret of Philip's influence lay in his supernatural sympathy. Nature had endowed him with a very tender heart, and grace had so increased and purified its sensibilities, that it was evident he had attained to that perfect charity, which, for the love of God, loves its neighbour as itself. Hence, in his discourse with others, he seemed to become so supernaturally united with them, that, completely forgetting himself, he placed himself, as it were, within their very souls, penetrating their most secret thoughts and feelings, and making those thoughts and feelings his own. He would weep for their sins as if he were himself guilty of them; he would discipline himself for sinners who were too hardened to do penance for themselves; he would wrestle in prayer for those who were struggling against God's grace; he would speak gently to the proud, and lovingly to those whose feelings the world had chilled; he would bear patiently with the thoughtless, and occasionally, though very rarely, he would be severe with those who could be managed by no other means. So varied were the devices he adopted with various characters, that the true characteristic of his system of treating souls, may be said to have been its variety. Thus, he was enabled to manage his penitents with a gentle tact, which often excited their own wonder; for the simple fact is, that though men may resist force, and turn a deaf ear to entreaty, the most hardened are forced to bow before the magic power of sympathy. The following examples will give some idea of his various modes of dealing with different characters.

A shoemaker, called Stefano, came one day to the oratory, and out of respect to the noble persons present, he placed himself on the furthest benches. He was a hard, worldly man, who had spent his youth in the army, following the lawless life of the soldiers of that day; and now he was full of bitterness, entangled in quarrels with all his neighbours, hating every one, and hated by all who knew him. But though he had thus placed himself behind his superiors, Philip's quick eye lighted on him; and a glance told him that poor Stefano's heart was not so hard as it seemed, but that he had turned it against every one because, by a chain of untoward circumstances, every one's heart had been turned against him. He accordingly went up to him, drew him courteously forward to a better seat, and after the prayers and sermons were over, he spoke to him in such a gentle, winning way, that poor Stefano was quite touched by kindness, to which he had long been a stranger. Philip invited him to return, and he could not but accept the invitation; and so, day after day, he came to St. Girolamo, till at last he was drawn to pour out his whole heart to Philip, and then, being persuaded to frequent the sacraments, he gradually got rid of his angry passions, and became another man. He was now as full of charity as he had once been of hatred, giving all his savings to the poor, spending his whole time in prayer, and continuing for twenty-three years regularly to attend the oratory. He lived in a little house alone, and, as he grew old, his friends remonstrated with him, saying that he might die suddenly without any one knowing, or being at hand to help him; but he replied, that he placed his trust in our Lady, and he was sure she would never forsake him. And so it appeared; for one night he was taken suddenly ill; but, though he was dying, he had strength enough to call his neighbours, who went for the priest, and, after receiving the sacraments, he departed in peace.

Another case was that of Giovanni Tommaso Arena, who was in the habit of coming to the oratory, A.D. 1562, for the sole purpose of turning the exercises into ridicule. Several persons remonstrated with him, but as he paid no attention to them, they complained of him to Philip. Philip, however, only answered: "Have a little patience, and do not doubt;" and so Giovanni Tommaso went on as before, making a joke of all that was said or done in the oratory, while Philip would not allow any one to correct him. Philip meanwhile did not forget him, but was constantly praying for him; till at last, being touched by constantly hearing the word of God, and by the grace which Philip's prayers procured for him, he began to feel compunction for his bad behaviour, and placed himself under Philip's direction. In course of time he entered the order of St. Dominic, and while still a novice, died a happy death.

Among those who were in the habit of coming to Philip's room, was a young nobleman, who, though he was not his penitent, was greatly attached to him. But it had been revealed to Philip that this young nobleman was accustomed, through false shame, to make insincere confessions. Accordingly, one day, when they happened to be left alone, Philip fixed his eyes on him, and looking him steadily in the face, began to weep. The young nobleman was not a little surprised at Philip's strange behaviour, and inquired the cause of his tears; but Philip did not answer a word. Still, however, he wept, turning on his young companion a look of such ineffable tenderness and compassion, that at last the nobleman began to think how he could possibly be the cause of those tears; and then his conscience accusing him of his sin, he too began to weep. Thus they stood for some time, neither of them able to utter a word; till at length the nobleman broke the silence by throwing himself at Philip's feet, and confessing to him the sins, which he had hitherto concealed from his ordinary confessor. Then Philip threw his arms around him, and embracing him most affectionately, said all that he could to comfort him; but the whole scene had so worked upon his loving heart, that he could not recover his composure till he had retired to another room, where he wept like a child. The young nobleman now made a general confession to his own confessor, after which, when he next came to see Philip, the saint said to him: "My son, though you have not confessed your sins to me, God has revealed them to me. Your look is changed since you were last here, and now you have a good countenance;" words which Philip often used in speaking of sinners who had returned to a state of grace. The young man begged Philip to pray God to give him true contrition for his sins; and at the same instant the greatest compunction seemed to be infused into him, though, till then, he had never known what true contrition or devotion was.

A similar case was that of Marcello Ferro, a young man of noble family, who, though he was in holy orders and held a rich benefice, dressed as a layman, and was devoted to the world. He happened one day to fall in with a young penitent of Philip's in the Church of the Minerva, and in the course of conversation the latter said to him: "One of the priests of St. Girolamo, called Philip, is in the habit of coming here for vespers and compline and if you speak to him, you will be a happy man." Just then, Philip came into the church, and Marcello and his friend having joined him, they proceeded together to the choir; where, as soon as Philip had placed himself on his knees, he covered his face with his hands, and to Marcello's surprise, began to weep and tremble, as was his wont when he was praying very earnestly. After compline Philip spoke kindly to Marcello, and invited him to come to the sermons at St. Girolamo. Marcello went daily for a fortnight; during which time Philip made no remark about his dress, but continued to pray for him, and to speak to him in a way calculated to rouse his conscience, till at last Marcello became ashamed of his secular dress, and laid it aside. He afterwards made a general confession to Philip, and in the course of the confession, Philip looked fixedly up to heaven, and beginning to tremble in his usual way, he revealed to him the inmost secrets of his heart; and then, as if he saw that Marcello had been moved by this extraordinary manifestation of God's grace, and yet was struggling with his own convictions, he threw himself on his neck, and folding him in his arms, said to him in a tone of tender and earnest entreaty: "My son, do not resist the Holy Spirit; God wishes you to be saved." Startled and overcome by such loving solicitude for his soul's welfare, Marcello yielded to the movements of divine grace, and, giving himself up entirely to Philip's direction, reformed his life, and in time became one of his most intimate friends.

Philip followed a different line with Pietro Focile, a young Neapolitan, who led a very irregular life, and was much given to buffoonery. One day he went with some friends to the oratory, dressed in a fantastic and extravagant way; but, from the moment he entered, he perceived that Philip fixed his eye on him, and he felt as if every glance of that eye was a sharp sword, piercing his soul and laying open his sins. However, he stayed through the whole of the exercises, and was so impressed by them, that, when he went out, his friends remarked that he was quite an altered man, and asked him what had come over him. In spite of all his efforts to turn into a joke the impression that had been made on him, he could not throw it off, and at the end of a week he returned to St. Girolamo, purposing to make a good confession. Philip, however, took scarcely any notice of him, but, after he had finished the other confessions, told him to go away and come back again some other day, for that he could not hear him then. Pietro accordingly went away, and returned the next day; but he was again sent away: and day after day he came, and each time he was sent back as before. But the oftener Pietro was sent back, the more anxious he became to return; till at last, after the lapse of two months, Philip being satisfied as to his steadiness of purpose, heard his confession. From this time Pietro continued to attend the oratory, and eventually became very devout.

But though Philip was generally so gentle, he could be very severe. There happened to be in one of the prisons a condemned felon, who could not be induced by any of the religious who visited him to make his confession. As a last resource, Philip was sent for. On reaching the prison, Philip found the unhappy man in the chapel, blaspheming and howling with despair; whereupon, going up to him, he seized him by the throat with supernatural strength, and threw him down on the ground, saying: "I forbid you to say another word." Scarcely had the command been uttered, than the miserable wretch became calm, and asked Philip to hear his confession, after which he applied himself devoutly to making his preparations for death.

Philip used the same severity with a young nobleman who was quite hardened in sin. One day, after reproving him for his hardness of heart, and threatening him with the pains of hell, Philip added: "But I see that I must come to facts with you. Kneel down, and put your head on my knee." The young man obeyed, and Philip said: "Look there, and see with your own eyes the torments which await you in hell." He remained for some time in this position: what he saw we know not; but when at length he raised his bead, he was a changed man. He made a good confession, reformed his life, and persevered in the service of God till his death.

But though Philip's first object was to draw sinners to the sacraments, his work did not end there. When he had brought them into the confessional, much still remained to be done; for their hearts might be so hard that they were incapable of contrition; or their consciences might be so seared by long years of negligence, that they had no distinct perception of the sins which they ought to confess; or it might be that they had been so long in the habit of going to the sacraments once a year, merely for form's sake, as a matter of worldly respectability, and because every one expected them to go, that they had become the slaves of human respect, and had not the courage to make true and unreserved confessions.

In order to enable him to meet these difficulties, our Lord bestowed on him the extraordinary gift of reading the hearts of his penitents, and of seeing in spirit what they were doing when absent from him; so that if they were not perfectly sincere, or if they failed from ignorance to make good confessions, he was able to correct them. This extraordinary gift was so well known to his penitents, that those who were conscious of having committed sin, felt in his presence as if they were in a fire; while, on the contrary, those whose consciences were at ease, seemed to be in Paradise. Also, if several of his penitents were talking together, and the conversation happened to turn on some subject which might prove an occasion of sin, they would instantly check themselves, saying: "We must take care what we are about; for Father Philip will find us out."

The following are some of the cases in which he made use of this extraordinary power. Rafaello Lupo, a young Roman, who led a very disorderly life, was one day taken by a friend to St. Girolamo and after the prayers and sermons were over, they went up to Philip's room, when the friend, wishing to induce Rafaello to reform his life, told Philip that he was going to attend the Oratory regularly, and wished beforehand to make a good confession. Rafaello was not a little surprised and indignant at his friend's words, for no such thought had ever entered his head; but not having the courage to contradict him, he knelt down and made a false confession. Philip perceived what he was about; and when he came to the end of the confession, he took his head between his hands, and pressing it tightly, said to him: "The Holy Spirit has revealed to me that there is not a word of truth in all that you have said." At these words, Rafaello was struck with compunction for his sacrilegious act; and Philip following up the impression by suitable exhortations, he yielded to divine grace, and made an unreserved confession of all the sins of his whole life. He continued to confess regularly to Philip, and after some time entered the order of Strict Observance of St. Francis.

Ettore Modio omitted to confess certain temptations, whereupon Philip said to him: "You have had such and such temptations, and are careless in driving them away; and what is worse, you do not accuse yourself of them."

To another penitent who was deterred by false shame from confessing some very grave sins, he said: "My son, you have not come to confession with a sincere intention, for you have omitted to confess such and such sins;" going through them one by one, with all their attendant circumstances, which, as the young man himself affirmed, Philip could not possibly have known except by Divine revelation.

Teo Guerra, of Siena, happened to be present one evening when Philip was talking and laughing with some prelates[9] who had called on him; whereupon Teo, who was a stranger in Rome, thought within himself that such merriment was not very becoming, and that Philip was not such a saint as people believed him to be. The next morning Teo went to confession to Philip, and said not a word about his rash judgment of the preceding evening. But when he came to the close of his confession, Philip said to him: "Be careful, Teo, always to go to confession with a sincere intention, and take my advice never to be restrained by respect to your confessor from mentioning any sin, however small it may appear to you. Why do you not confess that you were scandalized at me last night?" He then narrated the whole, as it had passed in Teo's mind; and Teo, seeing

---

[9] In Rome this title is not confined, as in England, to bishops, but is given to all those who hold various offices of a certain rank, and the offices which confer this dignity are called *prelatures* (prelature).

that he knew the secret thoughts of his heart, conceived a very high idea of his sanctity.

One morning one of his penitents stayed away from his usual confession, because he had some temptations which he was ashamed to confess, and when he came in the evening to the oratory, he remained in the background. But Philip called him up to him and said: "Why do you avoid me?" Then drawing him aside, he reproved him, and told him the temptations, with all their circumstances, thus filling him at once with wonder and compunction. To another, who had gone to confess a particular sin elsewhere, he said, when he next came to confession: "My son, you have committed such and such a sin, which you do not wish me to know; but God has revealed it to me." While another, who hesitated from false shame to come to confession, he drew aside, and said to him, in a gentle and affectionate tone: "Tell me, my son, why you do not confess such and such sins?"

Philip was also careful to correct those who, from forgetfulness or inadvertence, neglected to confess some sin, even though it might be a venial one.

A penitent having forgotten a sin of hatred of which he had been guilty, Philip said to him: "Have you not wished for some one's death?" And the other answering that he had, Philip, who saw that the omission had been accidental, gave him absolution without saying more.

Francesco della Molara having made a general confession, Philip said to him: "My son, did you not commit such and such a sin?" To which Francesco answering in the affirmative, Philip added: "Then why did you not confess it?" "Because," answered Francesco, "I thought I had confessed it before." Philip, however, assured him that he had not; and on thinking the matter over, Francesco remembered that he had omitted it.

After Maria Maddalena Anguillara, an oblate of Tor de'
Specchi, had finished her confession, Philip looked fixedly at
her and said: "Think again." She withdrew and examined her
conscience anew, when she recollected some sins that she
had before forgotten, and returned to confess them. Filled
with astonishment she said: "Father, as you see into my
conscience, pray tell me whether there is anything more."
But Philip answered: "You need not be uneasy; there is
nothing more." She afterwards doubted whether the whole
might not have been accidental, or whether Philip might not
have had some knowledge of her sins; but the next time she
came to confession, before she began he said to her: "Stop,
I will tell you your sins;" and then he went one by one
through all the sins that she had been about to confess.

In order to prevent persons from coming to the
sacraments from interested motives, he would often send
some of his penitents secretly to relieve them. During a
great scarcity, a woman came to confession in hopes of
receiving some of the bread which was distributed at St.
Girolamo; but Philip refused to hear her confession, and sent
her away, saying: "Go and God be with you: there is no
bread for you."

CHAPTER XII

HE FIRST STEP in the spiritual life is to avoid sin, and consequently, Philip's first care was to keep his penitents not only from open and great sins, but from all that was in the least degree sinful in God's sight. In this part of his work he relied chiefly on supernatural means of grace, such as the sacraments and prayer. It has been already told how he enabled one of his penitents to overcome his besetting sin simply by making him confess it each time he fell into it.

He led another to reform his life by inducing him to repeat daily the Salve Regina, and to kiss the ground while he said: "Tomorrow I may be dead;" while the great means by which he worked on the masses around him, was the prayers in the oratory.

As to the sacraments, though he wished his penitents to communicate frequently, yet he laid greater stress on their going to the sacrament of Penance. Most of his penitents went to Holy Communion on every great festival; some went once, others twice a week, and a few went every day; but he wished them all to go more frequently to confession than to communion; and thus many who did not communicate every day went daily to confession. All the members of the oratory were in the constant habit of confessing at least three times a week.

Philip attached scarcely less importance to his penitents avoiding the persons and places which might prove occasions of sin to them. Having heard that a young penitent of his had gone to a masquerade, he scolded him very severely, and insisted on his burning his mask, lest he should be tempted to go again. On another occasion, having persuaded a young man to give up an attachment to a lady, which might have cost him his life, he insisted so strongly on his not even passing her house, that the young man never did so for two years.

He also advised his penitents to avoid idleness, as being a frequent occasion of sin. When young persons were in his room, he would always find something for them to do, making them read a spiritual book, or bidding them string rosaries, or weave garlands of flowers; and if these occupations failed, setting them to sweep the floor, or make the bed, or remove the furniture from one place to another; caring little what they did, so long as they were not idle. It has been already told how he found occupation for so many of his penitents in the hospitals. Besides this, it was his custom to keep many of them out of idleness by taking them with him of an evening to the Dominican church of the Minerva, or the Capuchin church of St. Buonaventura, where they would join the monks in saying vespers and compline. On the vigils of great feasts he would return with them to the church for matins and lauds, and remain there the whole night in prayer and preparation for the morning's communion. As it was his object to draw, rather than force, people to devotion, he spared no pains to make these little excursions as attractive as possible, enlivening their walk to the church by cheerful and winning conversation. Often, too, he would be accompanied by Giovanni Animuccia, master of the Pope's chapel, who would bring several of the choristers with him; and when the monks began to chant, these singers would take their part, and render the devotions so attractive, that great numbers would be drawn to the church, and often the choir would be filled with secular priests and laity.

Philip also attached great importance to the cultivation

of a cheerful temper; for he said it was much easier to guide light-hearted persons than those who are given to low spirits, and that few things are so opposed to a true spirit of devotion as a melancholy disposition. If he saw any of the young persons round him looking otherwise than light hearted and cheerful, he would immediately ask them why they looked so sad, and, giving them a slap, would bid them be merry. At the same time he was an equal enemy to foolish joking and buffoonery, often warning his penitents against them, on the ground that they not only unfitted a person to receive any increase of devotion, but rooted out whatever devotion he might already possess.

The following story shows how much Philip valued light-hearted equanimity. One day there came to visit him two Capuchins, the younger of whom struck him as having a true religious spirit, and he therefore determined to try him. The young monk happening to spit rather rudely, Philip seized the opportunity to reprove him very severely, reproaching him with his bad breeding, ordering him to quit the room, and finally, as if he were in a great rage, pretending to be about to strike him on the head with his shoe. The young monk, however, took it all patiently, and was not the least put out, though the elder monk, who was of a melancholy temper, showed by his countenance that he was extremely discomposed by the mortifications, which were inflicted on his companion. Philip next bade the young monk take off his cloak, because he was not worthy to wear it; to which the other instantly assented, saying, that he was willing to go without a cloak, not only because he was not worthy to wear it, but because it was not cold, and he had eaten a good breakfast that morning. Philip then tried him in several other ways, and finally dismissed him as if he were highly offended with him. But, scarcely had the two monks reached the bottom of the staircase, then Philip called them back; and, as the younger one approached, he ran to meet him, embraced him, loaded him with caresses, and at last bade him adieu with the words: "My son, persevere in this lightheartedness; for it is the true way to make progress in the practice of virtue."

The young, however, were the peculiar objects of Philip's care; since, as he used to say, people generally carry with them to their graves the bad habits which they have acquired in their youth. His skill in managing young persons was very remarkable. He did not fall into the common mistake of showing his care of them by great strictness of discipline, and still less by requiring them to maintain an outward demeanour of grave decorum. His way, on the contrary, was to accommodate himself to their youth, and to join in their amusements, in order to draw them round him, and thus gain the opportunity of exercising an influence over them. He would often quit his prayers, and go downstairs to laugh and joke with the boys who came to see him. Sometimes, too, he would take them out for a walk into the country, where he would set them to some active game, in which he would at first take part, and when he saw them interested in it, he would withdraw, and, retiring to a little distance, would sit down and read the Gospels, or some spiritual book which he had brought with him; and then, while the children sported merrily around him, the old man would become so absorbed in heavenly contemplation, that not unfrequently he would fall into an ecstasy.

Often, too, he would set the boys to play at ball opposite his room, in order to prevent their going to places where they might fall into bad company; and, when one day the other people in the home scolded them for making such a noise, he only said to them: "Never mind what they say; amuse yourselves, and be merry; for the only thing which I want from you, is that you do not sin." On another occasion, a gentleman having expressed his surprise how he could bear the noise that they made, the saint replied: "Provided only they do not sin, I would willingly let them chop wood on my back."

He was also anxious that they should confess very frequently; and when several of them would come together to confession, he would set one of his older penitents to look after them, lest they should do each other harm by gossiping about their sins, or about what had been said to them in the confessional. He would not, however, allow them to go to Holy Communion as often as they confessed. When they asked his leave to communicate, he would answer: "*Sitientes, sitientes, venite ad aquas;*"[10] and then he would set them special devotions by way of preparation, and not unfrequently, when the appointed morning came, he would bid them wait some days longer, and go through other devotions; and thus he would go on putting them off from day to day till they were properly prepared. He would also recommend them to do something more than usual for four or five days after their communion; as for instance, to say five Paters and Aves, with their arms extended in the form of a cross, or to repeat one of the rosaries which he was in the habit of teaching them; "Because," said he, "the devil attacks us more violently on communion days than at other times; and, if we do not resist, we shall do great dishonour to the sacrament."

So great was Philip's reputation for the management of youth, that the Superior of the Dominican convent of the Minerva would often send his novices to spend the day with him, feeling sure that they could not but derive great profit from his society. On these occasions he would take them to some beautiful place in the country, where they would dine, and spend the day; and, when he saw these young religious

---

[10] You are thirsting, thirsting, come to the waters. -Editor.

enjoying their meal, he too would rejoice, and would say: "Eat, my children, and have no scruples; for it makes me fat to see you do so." Then, when they had dined, he would make them sit down on the grass in a circle round him, and would talk to them on spiritual subjects, telling them the thoughts of their hearts, exhorting them to the practice of virtue, and especially to perseverance in their religious vocation, which, he used to say, was one of the greatest blessings which God had conferred on them; adding, as if to give force to his words: "I say this with my whole heart." As he spoke, the novices would feel themselves inspired with fresh fervour; and in the evening they would return to their convent happy, and full of peace and joy.

There was, however, one period of the year which was fraught with peculiar danger to all classes of persons, and especially to the young. This was the Carnival, when all the world seemed to go mad after amusement.[11] Plays, balls, masquerades, races, filled up the round of day and night; the ordinary restraints of society were laid aside; every one did as he liked; men and women of all ranks, concealed under masks, committed acts which they would have blushed to have known; and so long as the Carnival lasted, it seemed as if the people of Rome had ceased to be Christians. The Carnival in Rome in Philip's time was infinitely worse than it is now; and he would not have fulfilled his mission if he had not done something to meet this great and crying evil. He knew it would have been too much to expect his penitents during the Carnival to shut themselves up at home, or to come to St. Girolamo for the ordinary grave

---

[11] Carnival (*carni vale*, or farewell to meat) took place the night before Ash Wednesday, and we now call such celebrations by the French name, *Mardi Gras* (Fat Tuesday). In an age where Christmas trees and presents had yet to come into practice this was as exciting in preparation and exuberant in expectation and memory as Christmas is now. -Editor.

routine of prayer and sermons. They had been accustomed from their very childhood to look forward to the Carnival; the anticipation of that happy season was one of the first things they could remember, and they could not part with it so easily. There is a time for everything; and if they prayed and listened to sermons during the rest of the year, surely they might fairly take this one week's innocent recreation; for they were resolved to keep clear of everything like sin, and meant only to mix in the merry crowd, and laugh and amuse themselves;—and there could be no harm in that. So the Romans, both young and old, would probably have argued, if Philip had preached them a grave lecture against the sins of the Carnival, or if he had tried to convince them of the danger of going, even with the best intentions, to places of sinful amusement. But he was too wise to waste his time by making the attempt; and instead of doing so, he set about the matter in his own sweet way, in which the cunning of the serpent mingled with the simplicity of the dove. The Romans expected to be amused during the carnival, and he therefore bethought himself how he could at once amuse them and keep them out of the way of temptation. He accordingly had musical meetings in the Oratory, and he set his penitents to act plays of a moral character, which served to keep them away from immoral places of amusement. But besides these, he had another grand device for carrying away thousands from scenes of sin and debauchery, and this was a pilgrimage to the Seven Churches.

The pilgrimage to these ancient basilicas has been already mentioned as an old devotion of Philip's, dating from his first arrival in Rome. While he lived in solitude he was accustomed to make the round alone; but from the time of his ordination he had invited some of his penitents to accompany him, his party at first being fifteen, then quickly swelling to twenty-five or thirty, and so going on gradually increasing with his increasing influence. Now, however, he determined to make these pilgrimages more public and general.

On the morning of the appointed day, Philip and a few of his spiritual sons started at an early hour for St. Peter's, whence they went to St. Paul's, which was the place of general rendezvous. Here the people were divided into bands, a father of the Oratory being appointed to each, and they set off in regular procession, meditating in silence on some given subject as they went along. When they had meditated as long as Philip thought their attention would last, music struck up, and the whole party joined in singing some psalm, or litany, or popular hymn; and then, if time still remained, they conversed together on some spiritual subject, taking care to avoid all vain or frivolous conversation. In this way they proceeded to St. Sebastian's, and thence to St. Stephen's, at each of which Mass was said, and great numbers communicated. After the Masses, they repaired to the vineyard of some noble family, the Massimi, or Crescenzii, or Mattei, where the people were ranged on the ground, and the provisions which had been brought with them were distributed, a piece of bread, an egg, a small piece of cheese, and some fruit, with weak wine and water to drink, being given to each; and while they dined off this frugal fare, the musicians played popular airs, or sang well known hymns, those of the party who felt disposed joining in chorus. After they had dined and were sufficiently rested, they set out in the same order as before, dividing their time between meditation, singing, and spiritual conversation. They proceeded thus to St. John Lateran, St. Croce, St. Lawrence, and St. Maria Maggiore, at each of which a sermon was preached, after the last of which, at St. Maria Maggiore, they separated, and returned to their respective homes.

These pilgrimages proved so attractive, that before Philip's death the number of pilgrims rose to two thousand. They were joined by a great many religious, especially the Capuchins and Dominicans, the latter of whom often sent their whole novitiate. They were also the beginning of a new life to many, who, having first joined them from curiosity, were so impressed with all they saw and heard, that they came to the sacraments and placed themselves under Philip's direction.

CHAPTER XIII

HOUGH PHILIP was at all times unremitting in the care with which he watched over his spiritual children, his paternal solicitude for them was redoubled when they were ill; for he knew that the devil would then be more on the alert to tempt them, while their own power to resist him would be diminished by physical weakness. When the illness was of a serious character, he would take his post in the sick man's room, and never quit it till either he was out of danger or had passed to a better world, but would stay by him, praying with him, comforting him, and directing him how to meet the varying temptations of that trying season. But besides these common acts of charity, God enabled him to render unusual assistance to the dying, by giving him an extraordinary power over the evil spirits who crowd round a deathbed; as if to show how priests and others who live in close union with God, may help the departing soul by their prayers, much in the same way as fond relations are wont to soothe their bodily sufferings by their tender watchfulness.

In the year 1558 two remarkable cases of this kind occurred. One was that of Father Persiano Rosa, Philip's confessor, by whose command he had become a priest. The day before he died, he was filled with fear, and sitting up in his bed he dashed himself from side to side, making the sign of the cross and crying out: "*Tu judica me, Deus, tu discerne causam meam.*"[12] At this moment Philip entered the room;

---

[12] "Thou, O God, judge me, Thou O God discern my plea." This is somewhat modified from Psalm 42 (43) which begins the Extraordinary form of the Mass. -Editor.

and as soon as Persiano saw him, he exclaimed, addressing him as he was accustomed to do: *"Sancte Philippe, ora pro me,"* adding: "drive away that fierce black dog which is trying to tear me. Help me and pray for me, that he may not devour me." Philip instantly bade all who were present join him in saying a Pater and an Ave, and scarcely had he knelt down than Persiano cried out: "Thanks be to God, the dog is going; he is running away, he is at the door." Then Philip rose and sprinkled the dying man and the room with holy water, after which the devil returned no more; and the next day Persiano departed in peace.

About the same time died Gabriello Tana, a young man who had been converted about two years before, since which time he had led a very devout life. At the beginning of his illness he clung most eagerly to life, and begged Philip to pray that he might soon recover; but Philip, to whom it had been revealed that he would die, answered: "I am going to St. Pietro in Montorio, to say Mass for you in the chapel in which the apostle was crucified. I wish you now to make me a present of your will, that I may put it into the offertory and offer it to God; in order that if it should please God to call you, and the devil should tempt you, you may be able to answer, 'I have no will; I have given it to Christ.'" Gabriello obeyed, and Philip went and said Mass for him.

After the Mass, Philip returned and found Gabriello quite an altered man; for instead of praying for life, he was constantly repeating: *"Cupio dissolvi, et esse cum Christo,"*[13] pressing his crucifix with loving fervour to his heart, and saying to his friends: "Believe me, this life is become hateful to me, for I long to die, that I may go to Paradise." Then turning to Philip, he added: "Hitherto, Father, I have asked you to pray for my recovery, but now I entreat you to ask our Lord that I may quit this miserable life as soon as

---

[13] "I desire to be dissolved, and to be with Christ." -Editor.

possible." Thus the day passed; and in the evening, Philip being about to go home, Gabriello said to him: "Father, I wish to go to Paradise: pray for me that I may have that consolation." Then Philip answered: "But if it should please God to let you suffer some time longer, would you not submit to His will?" But Gabriello replied: "Father, what do I hear? You know that I long to go to Paradise to see God, and I cannot stay longer in this life. Pray our Lord, then, that I may depart before five o'clock." Philip rejoined: "Do not doubt, you will have your wish; but I warn you to be prepared to fight the devil bravely, for he will attack you violently. Wherefore remember that you have given your will to Christ, and do not fear, for He will fight for you." He then told him, one by one, all the ways in which the devil would tempt him; after which he went home, leaving Tarugi and Giovanni Battista Salviati to watch by the dying man, and bidding them send for him if anything new occurred.

Scarcely had an hour elapsed when the devil began his attack on Gabriello. The first temptation was to presumption; for when the Litanies were being read and they came to the words: "*A mala morte libera me, Domine,*"[14] he smiled, and shaking his head, said: "He who has Christ in his heart, cannot die a bad death." But instantly perceiving the deception, he cried out: "Brothers, help me with your prayers, for what I have just said, was a temptation of the devil." Scarcely was this trial past than the devil made a second attack, by trying to prevent his uttering the name of Jesus, which he had been so desirous to invoke at the moment of death, that he had charged his friends not to fail to bring it to his memory. He long tried in vain to say the holy Name, and even when he said it he could not be persuaded to believe that he had done so; and this struggle lasted so long and was so dreadful, that his friends sent for

---

[14] "From a wicked death, deliver me O Lord." -Editor

Philip. The sight of Philip seemed to revive poor Gabriello; and when Philip held the crucifix before him, and several times repeated the name of Jesus, he was able to repeat it distinctly after him.

The next attack was on his faith; for he now seemed to be unable to utter the word "Credo;" and even when he pronounced it after Philip, it seemed to him that he neither said it, nor believed in the way in which he wished. Then Philip bade all who were in the room kneel down and repeat the Credo in a loud voice, telling Gabriello to follow them at least with his heart; and when he himself knelt down and prayed, the temptation ceased, and Gabriello began to defy his enemy, saying: "I will believe in spite of thee. Whether thou wilt or not, I will believe to all eternity."

After some time the devil made his last desperate attack, appearing to the dying man in such a terrific form, that he began to tremble, and cried out in agony and despair: "Alas! miserable me! how many sins! how many sins! Oh God! have mercy! Oh Father! drive away those black dogs that are standing round me." Whereupon Philip, laying his hands on Gabriello's head, said aloud: "Malicious spirit, hast thou power to do violence to the grace of God! These hands have this morning touched Christ. I therefore command thee in His name to depart from this place, and to leave this creature of His alone." Scarcely had the words been uttered, than the temptation ceased, when Philip said to Gabriello "My son, be comforted, and say, *'Discedite a me omnes qui operamini iniquitatem.'*[15] Fear not; for if you have sinned, Christ has suffered and paid the debt for you. Enter, then, into His side and into His sacred wounds, and do not be afraid, but fight bravely, for soon you will conquer." He then knelt down at the foot of the bed, and in a few minutes the dying man cried out: "Joy, brothers, joy! The dogs are going.

[15] "Depart from me, all ye who work iniquity." -Editor.

Father Philip is driving them away: look how fast they run;" pointing to the place where he saw them. After this, he continued to speak with great fervour and confidence, till at last Philip, fearing he would exhaust himself, bade him be still and place all his hope in Christ and in His precious blood, through which he had conquered the devil. The bystanders and the physicians thought that he would linger till the next day; but Philip said that he would die as soon as he changed his position. And so it came to pass; for in half an hoar he turned to the side on which Philip stood, when, placing his face on Philip's hands and invoking the name of Jesus, he expired, his countenance being so beautiful after death that he looked like an angel from Paradise.

Philip used to say, that persons who are ill ought not easily to believe that they will recover, as the devil often uses this delusion to prevent their preparing for death. He was also in the habit of advising those who visited them, not to talk much to them, but rather to help them with their prayers.

CHAPTER XIV

 lthough everything that Philip undertook prospered under his hand, it must not be supposed that all went smoothly with him. No one ever came to be a saint without suffering, and Philip had his full share of it. His life may be said to have been one constant exercise of patience, insomuch, that many persons who at first thought lightly of him, changed their opinion, and were induced to regard him as a saint, merely from seeing the frequent trials which he had to endure, and the wonderful patience with which he bore them. His trials, too, were not the less severe because they partook of the same hidden and humble character as his virtues, and were not calculated, like those of St. John of the Cross, and other great saints, to command admiration by their extraordinary intensity.

The weight of so many souls was in itself no light burden; and the peculiar character of Philip's mission increased the weight of the charge. Had they been religious, and he the general of an order, his authority would have been seconded by that of solemn vows, and more than half the battle would have been won, when they had passed through their novitiate and had made their profession. Or, had he been an itinerant missioner, preaching from town to town, waking men from sin, and then passing on to another field of labour, he might have rejoiced over the fruit which each day brought forth, and gone on his way, taking no thought for the morrow. But his position was far more trying; for, like a religious superior, he was tied down to one field of labour, and had committed to him the charge of

souls whom he was required to conduct through the whole
course of their earthly combat, and to train to degrees of
perfection not inferior to those of religious; and yet his
children were not bound to him by any vow or other
exterior tie. They were free to obey or disobey him as they
would; they might come or go as they liked; and while he
must stand by to watch and aid them as they were tossed
about on the world's troubled waves, or driven hither and
thither by the gusts of passion amid the quicksands of
temptation, he had no peaceful cloister to offer them as a
refuge, and no extraordinary authority to appeal to when his
own poor words proved too weak to hold them. Thus, he
was always placed at a disadvantage, and his work was one
of constant care, ever beginning and never ending. Though
he drew so many souls to God, yet his labour, like that of the
missioner, did not terminate with their conversion, but must
be continued to their life's end. Many came to the
sacraments for a time, but when their first fervour had
cooled down, returned to their former worldly or sinful
mode of life; and these were such a constant source of
anxiety to him, that we are told that whenever he missed
any of those whom he was accustomed to see around him,
he would send some of his other penitents to look after
them. Many, even of those who joined his congregation,
withdrew from it after their vocation had been proved, and
these defections were a double grief to his paternal heart.
And even those who were going on steadily and
satisfactorily, were not less on his mind; for, like a loving
father, he was always watching the countenances and
conduct of his children, and was ever on the alert to detect
the change which sin had brought over their features, or to
confront those whose consciences made them shrink from
his eye, or to break down the barrier which false shame and
untold sins would have interposed between him and them.

In this part of his work he received, it is true, great assistance from the extraordinary gifts of the Holy Spirit; but even the power which he possessed of reading the thoughts of others, often served to increase the anxiety which attended his task, since it prevented his being deceived by any false show of virtue, which might have satisfied an ordinary confessor.

Amidst these trials, his only strength and support were prayer, and his extraordinary confidence in God. When his sons were discouraged by the defection of promising members from the congregation, he would reassure them by saying, that if every one of them went away he should not care, for that God did not want men. Though he now lived in the midst of the busy world, he was almost as constantly in prayer, as when he spent his time in solitude in the Catacombs. In summer, it was his custom to retire both night and morning to a little room at the top of the house, or to the roof of the church, whence he could see nothing but the sky and the distant fields, and here he would spend many hours in mental prayer. In winter he used to pray for two or three hours every evening before a crucifix, on which the light was thrown from a dark lantern; and when he went to bed he would take his rosary and crucifix with him, in order that he might begin to pray as soon as he awoke, for he never gave more than four or five hours to sleep. Sometimes, after going late to bed, he would be found up at an early hour the next morning, and he would then say, as if in jest: "I slept very little last night. What does that mean? What does that mean?" And when the person to whom he spoke would answer: "Father, you were praying;" he would reply: "This is not a time to sleep, because Paradise is not for cowards." Often, too, when he had been interrupted in his prayers during the day, he would pass the whole or greater part of the night in prayer; and on these occasions, if nature rebelled, and he found it hard to prevent himself falling asleep, he would keep himself awake by tying and untying knots in a cord. If he was called away when he was in the midst of his prayers, he would instantly go and transact the business for which his presence was required, saying, that properly speaking, he was not quitting his prayers, but only leaving Christ for Christ; and when the affair for which he had been called away was concluded, he would return to his meditations, and so far from being distracted by the interruption, he would be only the more recollected and inflamed with Divine love by the work of charity which he had performed.

But besides these set times for prayers, he had acquired such a habit of praying at all times and in all places, that he seemed to fulfil literally St. Paul's injunction: "Pray without ceasing." When he was at his meals, or when he was dressing, or when he was out walking, he would often become so absorbed in prayer that he would remain immovable, with his eyes raised to heaven, so that those who were with him would be obliged to call his attention to what he was doing, or to the persons whom he was passing, and ought to recognize; and on these occasions it was often no easy task to recall him, and when, by dint of pulling his habit, they had succeeded, he would start and would be unable to speak till he had shaken himself, like a person waking from a deep sleep. Often, also, when his room was full of visitors, and various subjects were being discussed, his usual self-command would prove insufficient to prevent his raising his eyes and hands to heaven and giving vent to his feelings in deep sighs, though he always deprecated such manifestations of devotion in the presence of others. So constant was his habit of prayer, that his friends found it necessary to do all they could to distract him in the afternoon, fearing that the continued tension of his mind, would injure his health. At certain solemn seasons, or when some public or private affair pressed urgently on him, his fervent devotion would be visibly increased, and he would be even more than usually absorbed; as for instance, in Holy Week, when it was his invariable custom as soon as he had said his Mass on Holy Thursday, to place himself before the sepulchre, and to remain there immovable on his knees without taking any food, till the Mass of Good Friday was concluded. He would not transact any important business till he had had time to pray; and even when his opinion or direction was asked by his penitents or friends, he would pause for a minute to pray before he answered. Thus he acquired such confidence in prayer, that he used to say: "Whenever I have time to pray, I feel sure of receiving from God whatever favour I ask of Him;" and not unfrequently when he would remark to those around him: "I wish such a thing to turn out in this way, and such another in that," they would observe that they came to pass as he had said.

In return for this constant and loving application to prayer God granted him many extraordinary favours. The most remarkable of these was the appearance of Our Lord to him in the Host, under the following circumstances. The Dominicans had a cause of some importance pending before the Pope, and on its account they had the Quarant' Ore in their church of the Minerva. Philip went to pray there, and, as he was praying in a retired corner, he was observed suddenly to become transfixed, with his eyes riveted on the Blessed Sacrament and a smile on his lips; and the bystanders, supposing that he had fallen into a fit, carried him into an adjoining cell. On coming to himself he exclaimed: "Victory! victory! our prayer is heard!" Whereupon the prior perceiving that it was not a fit that he had had, pressed him to explain the meaning of his words. At first he refused to do so; but, after some time, overcome by the prior's entreaties, he said that he had seen in the Host our Lord Jesus giving His blessing to all who were present, and that, consequently, they ought to thank God for the victory that He had granted them. It afterwards appeared that the Pope had given his decision in favour of the Dominicans at the very time when Philip recovered from his ecstasy.

But besides the trials which were inseparable from the charge of so many souls, and the peculiar character of his mission, Philip had many other calls for the exercise of patience. It was only in the nature of things that such a work as his should excite great opposition. Parents would be angry when their sons, to whose talents they looked for the aggrandisement of their families, preferred the exercises in the Oratory, and the conversations in Philip's room, to attendance in the antechambers of princes and cardinals. Husbands would grumble when their wives began to frequent the sacraments, and introduced into their families a tone of devotion which put themselves to the blush. The pride of noble houses revolted when their most distinguished members took to waiting on the sick in the hospitals, and joined a rabble mob in singing litanies through the public streets. And even cardinals and prelates were displeased when Philip drew the most promising of their retainers away from their service into holy orders. But besides these and similar personal reasons for enmity, the spirit of the world rose against one who dared to despise the world and the world's ways. Wherever Philip's penitents appeared they were greeted with sneers and mocking inquiries as to what Father Philip was doing, what dainties he had had for breakfast that morning, and how many fat capons and basins of rich soup his fair penitents had sent him. Such jokes were to be heard in the palaces, in the shops, in the banks, in fact, everywhere. Rome rang with them, and that not for a few weeks or months only, but for many years, and it may almost be said, throughout Philip's whole life. Some called him mad, because he had a dog which he often carried through the streets; others said he was an old fool, or that he must be in his dotage; and even some of his own penitents, trespassing on his humility, treated him rudely, as one who was simple and ignorant. Thus, wherever he or his penitents went, those who feared not God made sport of them.

But this was not the worst; for often the malice of his opponents took a darker form, and the slightest pretence sufficed for the circulation of some calumny against him. A servant called Philip, who sometimes came to the Oratory, having been put into prison for scandalous conduct, the report spread through the city that it was the saint who had committed the crime, and been imprisoned. When he began the pilgrimage to the Seven Churches, he was accused of gluttony, and of having taken with him seven donkeys laden with tarts; while others charged him with trying to gain popular favour by an appearance of great devotion; and even some of those who lived with him at St. Girolamo, joined this outcry, and blamed him severely for bringing himself into such public notice. Some of the cardinals and prelates, too, credited the stories against him, and treated him publicly with contempt. On one occasion, when he went to speak to a prelate in behalf of Fabrizio de' Massimi, who had been wrongfully accused of a capital offence, the prelate not only would not listen to a word he had to say, but loaded him with reproaches. And at another time a cardinal, who happened to meet him in the street, stopped his carriage, and reproved him publicly. But on this occasion Philip turned the censure into praise; for, knowing that the cardinal had no bad feeling towards him, but had been deceived by others, he took the reproof with perfect meekness, and then going up to him, whispered a few words in his ear, whereupon the cardinal changed countenance, and, loading him with caresses, said aloud: "Go on with what you are now doing."

But all that was said or done had no power to disturb Philip's equanimity. When people told him what was reported about himself or the exercises in the Oratory, he either said nothing, or laughed, generally taking as a good joke the idle tales which circulated about himself. And when the calumnies were of a graver character, he would speak of them in a way which proved that he not only bore with his enemies, but that he sincerely loved them, going often to St. Peter's to pray for them, and bidding his penitents say a Pater and an Ave for them. Whatever occurred, he was never seen to be melancholy or downcast, but always appeared with the same bright and happy countenance. It seemed impossible to make him angry; for, even when he found it necessary to assume an appearance of anger with any one, the moment the delinquent was out of sight, his usual serenity returned; and so well was this known to those around him, that they used to say: "Let us say or do what we will, nothing can disturb Father Philip."

At last there came to pass what every one thought must trouble him extremely, even though he was a saint. Those who had taken offence at the pilgrimage to the Seven Churches, could by no means be induced to believe that Philip could be taking so much trouble simply for the love of God and the conversion of sinners; and, accordingly, when they found that his austere life gave the lie to their charges of gluttony and hypocrisy, they accused him of introducing new doctrines and devotions into the Church, and of having interested motives for drawing such crowds around him.

These things occurred A.D. 1559, when Paul IV was carrying on his reforms, and such a charge could not escape his vigilance. Philip was accordingly summoned before the Pope's Vicar-General, who, receiving him coldly, said to him: "Are not you ashamed of yourself, you who profess to despise the world, are not you ashamed to draw such crowds around you in order to win popularity, and to pave your way to a prelature by this pretence of sanctity?" He then proceeded to reprove him very severely; and at last he ordered him to hold himself in readiness to appear before his tribunal whenever he should be summoned, and he forbade him meanwhile, for the space of a fortnight, to hear confessions, or to hold the usual meetings at St. Girolamo, or to go about the streets with a crowd of followers, threatening to put him in prison if he disobeyed. Philip received the reproof with perfect meekness and humility, and, without attempting to defend himself, he only answered with simple frankness: "My lord, it is a matter of indifference to me whether I continue or abandon this work. I began it for God's glory, and I am prepared to give it up for the same motive. Behold me, then, quite willing to obey the commands of my superiors, whatever they may be." This gentle answer, however, was so far from appeasing the Vicar-General, that it only irritated him the more, for he looked on Philip's proffer of obedience as a further piece of hypocrisy; and he, therefore, replied: "You are an ambitious fellow; and you are doing all these things, not for the glory of God, but in order to make a sect for yourself." Whereupon Philip turned to a crucifix, and said: "Lord, Thou knowest whether I do these things in order to make a sect, or for Thy sake!" and, with these words, he took his leave.

This was a dreadful trial to Philip, and the more so, because it fell not only on himself but on his friends and spiritual children, who grieved bitterly over the interruption of their usual devotions. Still, even this trial could not ruffle his peace of mind. His only thought and care were to obey his superiors, and to pray to God to manifest His will. When he walked out, he forbade his friends to follow him, and even sent them off in the opposite direction; but in spite of all his efforts, they would not leave him, but, allowing him to pass on, would follow him at some distance. He would not permit them to murmur either against his accusers, or against the prelate under whose censure he was lying; but he bade them have patience and pray, for the truth would at last become manifest, at the same time encouraging them by saying: "This persecution is not sent on your account, but on mine, for it is God's will to make me humble and patient; and you may rest assured that as soon as I shall have derived from it the fruit which He purposes, and shall have been well mortified, it will cease."

Meanwhile he recommended himself to the prayers of all the most devout persons in Rome, and he and his friends never ceased to pray. One day, when they were in the Oratory, there came in a priest in a coarse habit, with a cord round his waist, whom none of them knew and whom they never saw afterwards; and he told them that he was come from certain religious, to bid them set up the devotion of the Quarant' Ore, for it had been revealed to them that great benefit would thereby accrue to their cause. He then went up to Francesco Maria Tarugi, and whispered in his ear, that the persecution would soon cease, and that Philip's work would afterwards be more firmly established and go on increasing rapidly; for that God would change the hearts of some of those who now opposed him, while those who continued obstinate against him, would come to an untimely end. Philip obeyed the command of the unknown priest, and set up the devotion of the Quarant' Ore; and before the fortnight had elapsed, God sent him the promised relief. He was once more summoned before the Vicar-General and some other prelates, and when he appeared, his judges began to question him as to his proceedings. He gave them the same answer as he had before given to the Vicar-General, telling them that he placed himself entirely at their disposal, and was prepared either to prosecute or to abandon his work, according as they should will. His judges had already discovered that most of the charges against him were frivolous and unfounded, and this meek answer so surprised and pleased them that they at once acquitted him, and gave him permission to hear confessions, and to resume the usual exercises at the Oratory, and the pilgrimage to the Seven Churches. The Pope also sent him two of the blessed candles which are burnt before his Holiness on the Feast of the Purification, with a message giving him full permission to go to the Seven Churches, and to continue all his exercises, bidding him pray for him, and that he only regretted that he himself could not join their devotions. It would be hard to describe what was the joy of all at St. Girolamo when the news of Philip's acquittal reached them, and how they blessed and praised God when the Pope's message was delivered. The Oratory was re-opened, the exercises were resumed with fresh fervour, and, by way of thanksgiving, a pilgrimage was made to the Seven Churches, when a much greater number of persons than before joined the procession.

It has been already narrated how, when Philip was a child, he made an attack of fever an opportunity for gratifying his desire of suffering joyfully for Christ's sake; and during the whole course of his life he continued to regard illness in the same light. This practice of virtue seemed to be so pleasing to God, that, as if to satisfy the cravings of his loving heart for union with his suffering Lord, God sent him very frequent attacks of illness, so that scarcely a year passed without his being dangerously ill. On these occasions he did not become low-spirited or fretful, but retained his usual cheerful look and manner, continuing his accustomed devotions, and conversing with those around him with such sweetness, wisdom, and composure that it seemed as if it was not he, but some one else who was ill. He uttered no word of complaint, and asked for nothing to ease his sufferings, but simply obeyed the commands of the physicians; and when he had their permission, he sought no other solace than hearing the confessions of his penitents. Even when he was in great pain or supposed to be dying, he would make no allusion to his own illness or sufferings, unless it were to utter from time to time words of such deep humility or tender love, that the hearts of those who stood round his bed of pain, could not but be inflamed with the love of God. Thus, he would often say: "If God restores me to health I will change my life and begin to do good," and, at other times he would exclaim, while he wept bitterly: "My Lord, if Thou wishest for me, here I am, my Love, for I do not yet know Thee, my God. Alas! miserable me! for I have never done any good."

In the year 1562 he had a more severe attack of illness than usual, brought on by excessive fatigue. It began with a pain in the nerves of his right arm, which became so acute, and was accompanied by so much fever, that he seemed to be fast sinking under it, and his life was despaired of by the first physicians in Rome. His spiritual children were overwhelmed with grief, and ceased not night or day to pray for him, some of them going from church to church, entreating God with tears to spare him, and others watching by his bedside, and deeming it their highest honour and greatest consolation to do the least thing for him.

Meanwhile Philip grew worse and worse, and it was thought necessary to tell him that the physicians had given him up. On hearing this he declared that he knew he was not going to die, for he had received so many benefits from

God, that he could not believe that He would call him to Himself while he was in a state so little fit to appear before Him; but he added, that though he was sure he would not die, he would not neglect to prepare himself for death. This he accordingly did, making a general confession and receiving the last Sacraments; but no sooner had extreme unction been administered, than the fever suddenly left him, and the pain began rapidly to subside. In a very short time he was completely restored to health, and his recovery was so wonderful that his physicians and those who were in attendance on him, declared his cure to have been miraculous.

CHAPTER XV

HILE GOD was thus employing Philip in reviving the faith and love of those within the bosom of the Catholic Church, it must not be supposed that the great desire which he had once felt to shed his blood in spreading the faith among those without the fold, was in the least diminished. His zeal for the propagation of the faith was as fervent as ever, and though it could find little scope in Rome, he made the most of the few opportunities which offered for its gratification.

The mere sight of a Jew moved him so deeply that he could not repress his sighs and tears, and would leave no means untried to effect his conversion. It has been already told how he converted by his prayers a Jew whom he met in the church of St. John Lateran. A similar case was that of two young Jews, whom Marcello Ferro happened to fall in with in the portico of St. Peter's. They fell into conversation, and Marcello, after drawing their attention to the two great apostles, who were Jews like themselves, succeeded in persuading them to accompany him to St. Girolamo. Philip received them with more than his usual cordiality, and so fascinated them by his affectionate interest in them, that they returned day after day to see him. This went on for several months, and Philip began to have good hopes of their conversion, when all at once their visits ceased. He now feared that their family might have interfered to prevent their carrying their good intentions into effect, or that they themselves might have been seized with sudden alarm at the greatness of the step which they were about to take; and he therefore sent Marcello Ferro to look after them, and to try to discover the cause of their sudden disappearance. Marcello went to their house, and saw their mother, who, not suspecting the secret motive of his visit, told him that one of them was dangerously ill, and asked him to go upstairs and see him. There, indeed, Marcello found the poor young Jew, apparently not far from death. He had refused food for some time, but he was so pleased to see Marcello, that his mother thought he might possibly take something from his hand, and asked him to make the experiment. This gave Marcello an opportunity of going quite close up to the invalid; and while he offered him some food, which the other instantly took, he whispered in his ear: "Father Philip desires you to remember him." On hearing Philip's name, the countenance of the young Jew brightened, whereupon Marcello added: "Remember you promised Father Philip to become a Christian." To which the other replied: "I remember it, and I will do it if God spares my life." On returning to St. Girolamo, Marcello told Philip all that had passed, and Philip answered: "Do not doubt. We shall help him with our prayers, and he will be converted." And so it came to pass; for in answer to Philip's prayers, the Jew recovered, and he and his brother were soon after baptized.

Philip also converted another Jew, a very rich man, who was baptized at St. Peter's. After his conversion this man continued to keep up a very close discourse with his father, which seemed scarcely prudent to the Pope, then Gregory XIII, who feared that his faith might be shaken by his father's influence over him; but Philip begged his Holiness not to interfere, for that he had a very certain hope that the son would convert the father. In course of time the father consented to accompany his son to see Philip, whose words had such an effect on him that soon after he also became a

Christian.

Many years after, A.D. 1592, this man received into his family four nephews of his, whose father was dead, and hoping that they would be converted, he took them frequently to see Philip. For some time Philip said nothing to them about their faith; but at last, one evening he begged them to pray to the God of Abraham, of Isaac, and of Jacob, to teach them to know the truth; adding, that he had already been praying for them, and that the next morning he would say Mass for them, and would pray so earnestly for them that they would be compelled to say "Yes." The next morning different persons argued with them for several hours, but they remained quite obstinate, till at length, while Philip was saying Mass, they seemed all on a sudden to be convinced, and consented to become Christians. One of them afterwards affirmed on oath, at the process of Philip's canonization, that he had been compelled that morning to say "Yes," because it seemed to him as if a spirit was whispering within him: "Say yes."

After this the young Jews went to stay at the Oratory, in order to be instructed preparatory to their baptism; and it came to pass that one of them fell dangerously ill, and on the sixth day he was in such an alarming state that the fathers were thinking of having him baptized at once. Philip then went to see him, and placing his hands on his forehead and his chest, he prayed for him for a considerable time, trembling, as he often did, from the vehemence of his devotion, after which he said: "I wish you not to die, because the Jews will say that the Christians have killed you; therefore, tomorrow morning send to remind me that I pray for you in my Mass." On hearing which, Father Pietro Consolini who was present, said to the invalid: "You will certainly be cured, because this holy old man has done similar things on other occasions."

During the night the young man became so much worse, that when the physician, Girolamo Cordella, came next morning to see him, he gave him up, and went to his uncle to tell him to lose no time in going to the Oratory, as his nephew was at the point of death. Meanwhile the hour came for Philip to say his Mass, and no sooner was it finished than the young man sat up in his bed, as if there was nothing the matter with him; and when his uncle arrived, expecting to see him dying, he found him without any fever and in perfect health. In the afternoon Cordella came to visit him; but as soon as he felt his pulse he made the sign of the cross, and said: "You have physicians in this house, and yet you send for those from without." And on going out of the house, meeting a fellow-countryman, Giovanni Battista Martelli, he said to him: "A wonderful thing has happened to me. This morning I visited a patient at the Oratory, who was at the point of death; and this afternoon, on my return, I found him so well, that I doubted whether the fathers were not deceiving me by substituting a person in health for my patient." Whereupon Martelli answered: "Certainly, it is a great miracle, and Philip is a great saint." About two months after, on the Feast of St. Simon and St. Jude, the four brothers were baptized by the Pope, Clement VIII, in the Church of St. John Lateran.

Philip inspired his penitents with a similar zeal for the conversion of Jews. One of them, Francesco Maria, generally called the Ferrarese, happening once to see a Jew, was so touched with compassion for him that he began to pray daily for him; and he prayed with such fervour and perseverance, that at last God granted his petition in a most unexpected way. After he had thus prayed for this unknown Jew daily for three years, he chanced one morning to be in St. Peter's, when a Jew was brought thither to be baptized; and on going up to him he found, to his great joy, that it was the same for whom, though a stranger to him, he had been so charitably praying for these three long years.

Heretics also were especial objects of interest to Philip, and his zeal for the faith led to the conversion of many of them. Among others was one called Paleologus, a man of some note in his sect, who had been imprisoned as a teacher of heresy, and for other capital crimes. While he was in prison every means had been tried to convert him, but he continued obstinate, and was at last sentenced to be burnt in the Campo dei Fiori. On the appointed morning Philip was in the confessional, when news was brought to him that the unhappy man was being led out for execution, on hearing which he instantly left the confessional and went to meet him, hoping by a last effort to avert the imminent danger which threatened his soul. He came up with the crowd in one of the adjoining streets, and, making his way boldly through the guards, he went up to the prisoner, and throwing his arms around him and pressing him to his breast, he said to him in the tenderest accents all that was most calculated to waken him to repentance. Nor were his words thrown away; for on reaching the Campo dei Fiori, Paleologus asked: "Where is that old man who spoke to me just now with such evangelical simplicity?" Philip was accordingly called, and resumed his efforts to touch the heart of the heretic, continuing them till they reached the stake. Then, as if moved by a sudden inspiration, he ordered the escort to stop, and forbade the executioners to proceed with their duty; and such was the reverence which the saint inspired, that they could not do otherwise than obey. He then made Paleologus mount upon a bench and recant all his errors publicly, after which he had him led back to prison. Here he continued to visit him, instructing him, and giving him the "Lives of the Saints" to read, because, as he said, their example was better calculated than learned arguments to subdue the pride and arrogance which generally lie at the root of the errors of heresiarchs. Paleologus seemed for a time to derive profit from Philip's instructions, though Philip often said that he was not satisfied with his conversion; but at last he began to vacillate, and fell back into his old errors, and after two years he was again condemned to death. Philip now spared neither tears nor prayers to save his soul, and at last brought him to repentance, in which state he was beheaded as a lapsed heretic, being assisted in his last moments by two of Philip's sons, Francisco Maria Tarugi and G. F. Bordino.

The same zeal for the propagation of the faith led Philip at various times to set his sons to write books which were calculated either to confute the writings of heretics or to confirm the faith of Catholics. He set Baronius to write Annotations on the Roman martyrology, and Tommaso Bozzio, a book called *"De Signis Ecclesiæ Dei,"* and Antonio Gallonio, the "Lives of the Saints." But the work which has immortalized Philip's zeal for the faith, is "Baronius' Ecclesiastical Annals."

About this time the Protestants published the "Magdeburg Centuriators," which professed to be a history of the Church from apostolic times, and to prove that the faith of the Catholic Church is not that of the Apostles. Philip, perceiving how likely this book would be to mislead simple and ignorant persons, became very anxious that a true history of the Church should be published, in refutation of the false statements of the heretics; and after much prayer and thought, he came to the conclusion that it was the will of God that Cæsar Baronius should carry out his idea. Baronius was in the habit of preaching in the Oratory on death and hell, and rewards and punishments, dwelling on God's justice in a tone of stern severity little in accordance with Philip's gentle spirit; and Philip, therefore, recommended him to change the subject of his sermons, and to relate the history of the Church, year by year, from the birth of our Lord to his own time. Baronius, however, had his own views about the matter, and disregarding Philip's advice, he continued to preach as before. Philip renewed his suggestion but Baronius had such a repugnance to narrating the history, that he paid no heed to Philip's words; and so it went on for a considerable time, Philip urging on the work, and Baronius shrinking back from it, till, at last, Philip, finding that he could not carry his point in his usual gentle way, laid a positive command on Baronius to begin it. Baronius was now in great perplexity, for on the one hand, he did not wish to disobey Philip, and, on the other, the task appeared to him so great, and was so opposed to his natural tone of mind, that he could not hope to succeed in it. At length, however, he had a dream which decided the point, for he dreamt that he was with Onofrio Panvino, who was then collecting materials for a Church history, and that he was telling him the task which Philip had imposed on him, and was begging him most earnestly to perform it for him. But it seemed to him that Onofrio would not listen to him, but kept turning away from him, whereupon he pressed him the more warmly; and while he was doing thus, he heard most distinctly the voice of Philip saying to him: "Be quiet, Baronius, and do not trouble yourself in this way; for you, and not Onofrio, must write the ecclesiastical history." From this time Baronius felt satisfied as to our Lord's will, and he at once set about the task assigned him. He went through the history of the Church from the birth of Our Lord to his own time; and whenever he came to the conclusion, Philip bade him recommence it; and thus he continued for thirty years to narrate Church history in the Oratory, going through it seven times before he published the first volume of his Annals.

Most people, when they had set a young man to a work of such importance, which would occupy a long life, and which he would possibly never live to finish, would have done all in their power to lighten his other duties, and to remove all other calls on him, in order that he might thus devote his whole time and talents to the one object. But Philip did the very contrary of this. He knew how engrossing intellectual pursuits naturally are; and he was aware that the satisfaction which Baronius would feel as his work grew under his hand, might easily degenerate into self-complacency, while thoughts of self might unconsciously mingle with his hopes of doing service to the Church; and therefore, instead of confining him exclusively to his great task, he acted as if it had been his aim to hinder him at it. Though he was always urging him to advance more rapidly with his history, he would not permit him to neglect his ordinary duties for his studies, but compelled him to attend the Oratory, and preach, and visit the sick, and be at the beck and call of every one who came to St. Girolamo; and some years after, when the congregation was formed and he was ordained, he not only required him to be always prepared to hear confessions, and to take his turn with the others in community duties, but appointed him superior; so that there was not an hour in the day which was free from interruptions, and in which he was not liable to be called from the most intricate historical researches to attend to some petty household detail, or to some ordinary spiritual office, which any one else in the house was equally competent to have performed. It was in vain Baronius complained of such needless interruptions. Philip would listen to no remonstrances, and seemed deaf to all reason, but persevered in throwing all sorts of obstacles in his way, while at the same time he would receive no excuse for the slow advance of the work. There was only one favour which he would grant him, and that was, that he should choose his own hour for saying Mass, but he insisted that he should be punctual to the hour which he had selected, and should quit his studies the moment the sacristan summoned him. He gave him also but one reward for his labours, and that was, that on each occasion when he completed a volume and brought it to him, he laid on him an obedience to serve thirty masses, just as if he had been the least and lowest in the house. When one considers what a gigantic work the composition of the Ecclesiastical Annals was, one is inclined to wonder how, with all these interruptions, Baronius ever accomplished it. He, however, lets us into the secret in the preface to the eighth volume of the Annals, which appeared soon after Philip's death, and which he dedicated to the saint.

"You constantly watched over me, urging me on by your presence, pressing me with your words, always exacting most rigidly, pardon me if I say it, what you required from me day by day; so that it appeared as if I had committed a sacrilege, when occasionally I strayed to anything else, for you could not bear that I should turn for a moment from the task you had laid on me. Often, I confess, I was half scandalized; for it appeared to me that you were acting tyrannically towards me, because I was measuring only my own strength, and was not considering that you had in silence arranged it all with God. Thus, too, as it happened to the children of Israel in Egypt, whose task was increased while straw was denied them, many other things were required from me, the care of souls, and preaching, and the government of the house, and many other duties were daily imposed on me by one or another; and consequently it seemed that by acting thus, or allowing others to do so, you were asking from me everything else except that which, above all, you wanted of me. But in this it appeared that you were only imitating Elias, who, when he wished to conquer the priests of Baal by calling down fire from Heaven to consume his sacrifice, first caused the altar to be bathed three times with four buckets of water, in order that the power of God might be the more manifest.

"And on the other hand, while you were helping me with your prayers, you laid your hand on the work, and it then seemed that you were imitating Eliseus, who, having laid his hand upon the hand of the king, caused him, in shooting the arrow, to be the conqueror of all Syria. So you, by doing the like, added your strong hand to my weak one, and converted my dull style into an arrow of the Lord against the heretics. Which as I know it to be true, it is also most pleasing to me to declare openly."

Cæsar Cardinal Baronius

CHAPTER XVI

HE FAME OF PHILIP'S work and of his sanctity was not long in reaching his native country. Thus it came to pass that, about six years after the commencement of the exercises at St. Girolamo, the Florentines offered him the charge of their Church at Rome, generally known as St. Giovanni dei Fiorentini. At first Philip declined their offer, because, he said, he could not make up his mind to leave St. Girolamo. The Florentines, however, laid the matter before the Pope, Pius IV, and on his expressing a wish that Philip would accept the charge, he hesitated not to obey, stipulating, however, that he should not be obliged to give up his residence at St. Girolamo. There was little difficulty in carrying out this stipulation, because Leo X had established a confraternity of ten priests under a superior at St. Giovanni, A.D. 1519, and Philip had, therefore, only to look out for priests to work under his direction.

With this view, he caused Cesar Baronius, Giovanni Francesco Bordino, and Alessandro Fedeli to be ordained priests, and sent them, together with Giacomo Salorti and Giovanni Rausico, to live at St. Giovanni. Rausico had charge of the parish; but neither he nor Salorti had any connexion with the Oratory. After a short time they were joined by Tarugi and Angelo Velli, and by two youths, Ottavio Paravicini, and Germanico Fedeli, nephew to Alessandro. Philip drew up for them a few simple rules, which, however, bore no resemblance to the constitutions of a religious order, but were expressly intended for secular priests living together without vows, the chief obligations being, meals in common and obedience to the father superior. It was a beautiful sight to see these fathers living together as if they were animated by only one will, while no words can describe the tender love and solicitude with which Philip governed them, ever watching over their souls, and urging them onwards in the path of perfection. He seldom had recourse to authority, but depended chiefly on paternal admonition and affectionate persuasion for inducing them to do what he would, wishing to lead them by love, and not by fear; and in this way he effected more by entreaties than others could have done by commands. As for his sons, they loved and revered him as their guide, their pastor, and their father; and the only wish of their hearts was to walk in his footsteps, imitating his humility, and taking the tone of their spiritual life from the perfect example which he constantly set them.

They took it in turn to wait at table, and for some time each took for a week the office of cook, vying with each other in performing the lowest duties, and loving to obey rather than command. Even Baronius was not excused on account of his intellectual labours; so that it often happened that, when learned men came to speak to him, they found him in the kitchen with an apron tied before him, washing the saucepans; nor did he desire an exemption from these menial occupations, for he left inscribed on the kitchen chimney-piece: "*Cæesar Baronius, coquus perpetuus,*"[16] as a record of the cheerfulness with which he took his turn in the office. During their meals, either Germanico Fedeli or Ottavio Paravicini read aloud, first out of the Bible, and then out of some spiritual book, after which a moral doubt was proposed, and each in turn gave his opinion. At a later period, when the congregation was formally established, three books were read, and two doubts were proposed at

---

[16] "Caesar Baronius, cook forever." -Editor

each meal.

The fathers went to St. Girolamo every morning to confess to Philip, and returned thither in the afternoon for the sermons, and again in the evening for the prayers; but from this time the usual oratory exercises were discontinued on Saturday, because on that day all the fathers were engaged in sweeping and cleaning the church. On Sundays and other festivals some of them heard confessions, while the others gave Holy Communion, after which they sang High Mass; and Baronius and Bordino took it in turn to preach, wearing their cottas, to please the Florentines, though it was their custom to preach at St. Girolamo only in their habit. Hence, when the Oratory was formally established, it became the practice for the fathers to preach in cotta, only on Sundays and festivals, and in their habit on other occasions. In the afternoon of these days they sang vespers in choir, and then went to meet Philip at the Minerva, or some other appointed place, where he would hold spiritual conferences, proposing some subject, and then calling on first one and then another of those who were present to give their opinions. These chance afternoon meetings gradually led to the custom, which became established in the Roman Oratory, of going after Easter to Mount St. Onofrio, a fine open spot commanding a view of the city, or in the heat of summer to some church more within reach; in which places they would begin by singing a hymn, after which a boy would recite a short sermon, and some of the fathers would speak briefly on spiritual subjects, while, in order to enliven the tone of the meeting, music would be introduced between the discourses and at its conclusion. In winter these meetings were held in the Oratory, when the usual prayers were said, the Litany and Antiphon of our Lady were sung, the short sermon was recited by a boy, and one of the fathers preached for half an hour, music being introduced as usual, both before and after the sermons. On these occasions great crowds were drawn thither by the novel and cheerful tone of the devotions.

Such was the origin of the congregation of the Oratory, though many years had yet to elapse before it took a regular place in the Church. At the period of which we are now speaking, it was only a family of brothers dwelling together in beautiful harmony, and united by the bond of love to one common father, whose slightest word or look had more power over them than the most stringent rule could have had. The spirit of their father seemed to rest on them, and aided by his prayers, they performed at St. Giovanni a work scarcely inferior to that which he was carrying on at St. Girolamo. The edifying spectacle which they presented, led, in course of time, to many persons of rank and learning asking for admission into their community, but Philip accepted only such as were truly humble and devout. High dignities were also forced on some of them much against their will. Bordino was made bishop of Canaglione A.D. 1592, and archbishop of Avignon A.D. 1596; Baronius held the offices of protonotary and confessor to the Pope, and was made a cardinal A.D. 1596; Tarugi, after founding the Naples Oratory, was made archbishop of Avignon A.D. 1593, and a cardinal A.D. 1596. But so dear was St. Philip's rule to his sons, that both Baronius and Tarugi returned to die in the congregation. Ottavio Paravicini also became a cardinal; and many other dignities were held by those who joined the community within the first few years of its existence.

CHAPTER XVII

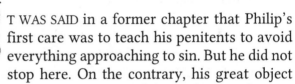 T WAS SAID in a former chapter that Philip's first care was to teach his penitents to avoid everything approaching to sin. But he did not stop here. On the contrary, his great object was to train them to the practice of the highest perfection, according to the measure of grace which God had given to each.

It was not, however, a religious perfection to which he sought to lead them. Many who came to him had religious vocations, and, knowing that his mission lay not with them, he sent them into various convents, so that there was not an order in Rome to which he had not sent novices. But his own field of labour was a wider one, and therefore it behooved him to mould his system with a freer spirit than that of the cloister. As his mission lay with the great mass of Christians living in the world, no strict external rule would have embraced the infinitely varied characters and needs of those committed to his charge; and consequently his only rule was that of the Church and of charity; the only spirit by which he worked was that of love; and in training his children to the practice of virtue, he did not set before them a narrow or exclusive ideal of perfection, but rather sought to breathe into them a generous and loving spirit, which alone would suffice to lead them safely through the world's thorny and chequered paths.

Philip had perfected his own views of Christian virtue during his vigils in the catacomb, and therefore the ideal which he set before his penitents was akin to that of the Church in the days of her first love, when each of her children stood prepared to quit family, and home, and wealth, and honour, and even life itself, at any moment that their Lord might turn to them and say: "Lovest thou Me more than these?" It is often easier to part at once with what we love than to retain and enjoy it, and yet to hold it so loosely that it may be taken away without the least struggle or resistance; but this was the very kind of detachment which God required from the ancient martyrs and confessors, and which He still generally requires from those who live in the world, and therefore it was to this that Philip aimed to lead his children. He did not require them to sacrifice their domestic ties, or their worldly possessions, or the natural characters which God had imprinted on each, but he taught them to be ready to part, without limit or reserve, with whatever our Lord might ask of them; knowing well that when our Lord is drawing a soul closer and closer to His Sacred Heart, He will sanctify first one affection, and then another, and then another, till all that is inordinate, and all that opposes the operations of Divine grace, shall have been removed, and the soul is left void, to be filled with Divine love alone.

Philip made so much account of detachment that he used to say, that if he could find ten men who were perfectly detached he should not be afraid to undertake to convert the world. Perfect conformity to the will of God he considered to be the best means of attaining this virtue; and he was so constantly in the habit of bringing the Divine will before his penitents, that the practice of this conformity may be said to be one of the characteristics of his system.

His constant prayer was: "Lord, if Thou requirest nothing from me, make me to know it, and I will never move or do anything of myself;"[17] and the same principle regulated his guidance of others. He did not impose on his

---

[17] *Life of the Venerable Mariano Sozzino,* l. 2, ch. 4.

congregation or his penitents a strict distribution of time, resembling the daily rule of conventual life; but he left them free to follow from hour to hour the calls of God, and to look for His guidance, not only in great things, but also in the most minute circumstances of their daily life and occupations.

It was on the same principle of conformity to the Divine will that he required his penitents to regulate their social relations and duties. When Giovanni Battista Salviati wished to lay aside the dress and retinue which were common among persons of his high rank, Philip objected, because they befitted the station in which God had placed him, and he had no sufficient ground for believing that it was God's will that he should quit his position in society. When he was told of a woman who spent her time in prayer, and was said to have received extraordinary favours from God, his only answer was: "Let her attend to her spinning;" for he always doubted the reality of supernatural gifts, which were not united with the performance of the ordinary duties which have been imposed by God, and in which His will is unequivocally declared.

Philip enforced his precepts by his example. Being once asked to pray for a member of the congregation who was dangerously ill, he reflected for a few minutes, and then refused to pray for his recovery, because he had ascertained that it was God's will that he should die.

Antonio Regattiero asked him to pray for his wife, who was ill; but Philip, knowing that it was God's will to take her to Himself, gently said to the anxious husband: "Let her go, and do not take it to heart."

Virgilio Crescenzi, being slightly indisposed, Philip said to Costanza, his wife, that she must be resigned to the will of God; whereupon Costanza, understanding that her husband was going to die, threw herself at Philip's feet, and besought him with floods of tears to pray for his recovery. But though Philip's tender heart bled for the disconsolate wife, he could only answer: "It is God's will. Can you desire anything except what is for the good of your husband's soul?" And even when the poor woman brought her young children to his feet, and together with them renewed her entreaties, his only answer was: "It is for the good of Virgilio's soul that he should die now;" well knowing that the will of God is always the best for His children.

Giovan Angeli Crivelli having come to confession on Holy Thursday in perfect health, Philip looked fixedly at him, and said: "My son, go and pray for some time before the crucifix, and then return to me; for God wants something of you." To which Giovan Angeli replied: "Let His Divine Majesty do what He will, for I am ready to receive everything from His hand." Philip rejoined: "But if it pleased God to lay a very heavy affliction on you, would you bear it willingly?" "Trusting to His aid, I would bear it most willingly," replied the other. "Then see that you stand prepared," added Philip, "for, during the Easter festival God will call you." So Giovanni Angeli went away in peace, with no will but the will of God; and that evening he was attacked with a fever, which in four days carried him to a better life.

But though this waiting on the will of God suffices so long as God asks for nothing more, yet there will often occur cases in which some voluntary sacrifice becomes necessary, because obedience to the inspirations of grace are opposed to some human affection or domestic relation; and on these occasions Philip hesitated not to carry out the same unreserved conformity to the Divine will, regardless of every consideration which natural affection, worldly prudence, or human reason might urge against it. When, as has been already related, a lady told him that her husband was displeased because she had of late become more devout, and had begun to frequent the sacraments, Philip required her to trust in God, and to continue her accustomed devotions without heeding her husband's displeasure. He prophesied that her husband would soon be more devout than she was; and so it turned out in the end. Again, when Baronius's parents objected to his following the devotional practices to which the grace of God had led him, Philip recommended no compromise, but encouraged Baronius to choose the better part, and to relinquish his domestic ties in order to follow Christ in the way in which He was conducting him.

The case was similar with the members of the congregation, for God had called them out of their several families, and had placed them in a new home, and given them fresh ties of filial and fraternal affection; and therefore, while Philip left them free to retain their natural kindred, he lost no opportunity of leading them gently on to imitate his own perfect separation from his home and family. We are told that Niccolo Gigli, a Frenchman, was so dead to all domestic affections, that when he received letters from his family he threw them into the fire without reading them; in return for which sacrifice of earthly love God granted him so large a measure of grace, that after his death Philip honoured as relics whatever had belonged to him.

Philip was so anxious that the members of the congregation should detach themselves perfectly from all natural ties, that, though he did not forbid them to visit their native country or their family, he constantly dissuaded them from doing so, even under pretence of changing the air for their health; saying: "That devotion is relaxed and lost among relations, and that nothing is gained by going among them; for that, on returning to the congregation, they would be sure to feel a repugnance to resuming their accustomed devotions and their former life, with all its restraints. He wrote as follows to one young man, who had entered the Oratory with good hopes of making progress in virtue, but who, contrary to Philip's advice, had gone with a friend, for change of air, to his native country, whence he never returned. "I wish," he wrote: "that N— had not left you so soon, and that you had stayed a shorter time in the midst of flesh and blood, and the love of mother and brother; for I have no doubt of this, having before me the example of St. Marcus and St. Marcellianus, who, though they had borne so many tortures, at last, moved by the love of father and mother, were near denying Christ, if St. Sebastian had not confirmed them by his words:— However, it depends on yourself either to remain or to return, for here we want no one by compulsion." He also tried to prevent Father Giovanni Antonio Lucci from going to Bagnarea, his native place; saying to him: "Giovanni Antonio, do not go away, for I know what I am saying," adding: *"Puto ego quod spiritum Dei habeam."*[18] Notwithstanding, Lucci went, and, being captivated by home and its endearments, he never returned to the congregation. It was remarked that of those of his sons who went to their own homes contrary to his wish, some died, and the rest never returned to the congregation.

Nor did Philip teach a less perfect detachment from worldly possessions, which are often found to hold the heart even more firmly than family affections. When the constitutions of the congregation were being drawn up, an article was inserted to the effect that the members were to give up their private property, as is usual with other religious bodies; but he erased the words, and wrote over them: *"Habeant, possideant,"* insisting that each should retain his private fortune. But at the same time he set them such a beautiful example of perfect poverty, and breathed into them

---

[18] "I reckon that I have some spirit of God." -Editor.

such a spirit of charity, that they truly imitated the detachment of those early Christians, who looked on their wealth as belonging to the Church, and themselves as treasurers and stewards for their Lord, holding it for Him, and dispensing it among His poor.

As for Philip's own example, he never departed from the life of poverty which he had embraced, when he relinquished his uncle's inheritance and turned his back on St. Germano. From that time he never received anything from his family, except one or two shirts from his father; and, when his father died and left him the life-interest of his property, he refused to accept it, and made it over to his sisters. His sister Elizabeth once sent him two shirts, which, however, were lost on the road, but he wrote to forbid her ever again to send him anything. While he lived with Galeotto Caccia, and afterwards at St. Girolamo, he refused to receive any pecuniary allowance; and, when his penitents offered him money, which they frequently did, he either declined it absolutely, or accepted it only for the service of the Church or the poor. He would have nothing to do with legacies, and refused to visit in their illness, those who had made wills in his favour; or, if he could not prevent the bequest, he either made it over to the heirs or took no notice of it. For instance, when Father Costanzo Tassone died, he left him a considerable legacy, of which a memorandum was given to him; but the only use Philip made of the paper was to cover a jar which happened to be in his room, as if to show the contempt in which he held such things.

In training his penitents to be indifferent to worldly possessions, Philip used often to say: "Let the young beware of sins of the flesh, and the old of avarice, and then we shall all be saints;" often remarking, that it is easier to convert the sensual than the avaricious. He often reproved those who were inclined to avarice, by saying: "He who wishes for riches will never have devotion;" and, if such persons asked his leave to fast, he would answer: "No, give alms instead."

At that time many priests used to receive money from those who came to confession; but Philip forbade the priests of his congregation to receive even the smallest sum, saying, that they could not get possession both of the soul and the purse, and if they wished to gain souls they must let purses alone.

He once asked Egidio Calvelli, a brother of the Oratory, whether he wished for money; and Egidio answering, "No, father, I have no wish for anything of the sort;" he replied: "In that case we can go to Paradise together; and I will myself lead you thither, but only on condition that you constantly pray to God never to let you wish for money."

Perceiving that one of his penitents had been eagerly scraping together a small sum of money, he said to him: "My son, before you had this money you had the face of an angel, and I liked to look at you; but now your look is quite changed; you have lost your cheerfulness, and are melancholy. Look, then, to your state." These words made the other blush, and so touched his heart, that from that time forth he gave up the pursuit of earthly wealth, and made it his sole study to lay up a treasure in heaven.

Francesco Zazzara, another of his penitents, was studying law, and hoped to rise to a distinguished position in society. But Philip called him one day, and making him kneel down, began to caress him in an unusual way, at the same time revealing to him his secret ambitious thoughts, and saying: "Happy fellow that you are! — you are studying now; and after you become a doctor you will begin to make money, and will advance the fortunes of your family; you will be an advocate, and perhaps one day you will get a prelature;"—and so, going on, he laid before the young man all the great things which the world could give, or of which he had ever dreamt, concluding with: "What a happy fellow you will be! then you will condescend to no one." Francesco was overjoyed at these fair promises, for he thought that Philip spoke in sober earnest; but at length the Saint stooped down and whispered in his ear: "And then?" These words struck him so forcibly that he could not throw off the impression they had made, but kept constantly repeating to himself; "I am studying in order to get on in the world—and then?"—till at last he turned his thoughts entirely to God, and giving up his studies, became a priest, and entered the congregation.

CHAPTER XVIII

ut though detachment from family affections and worldly possessions are great steps in the path of perfection—and there are few who live many years without being called by God to make some sacrifices of this kind,—yet there is another class of virtues which are even more essential; and these are humility, obedience, and all that may be included within the wide range of interior mortification. The occasions which call for detachment from family and wealth, generally occur but rarely and at long intervals, and some persons are never required to make such sacrifices, but every Christian is called on daily to detach himself from self; from pride, self-will, and self-love, under all its varied phases; and hence the practice of this interior mortification may be said to be the true school of detachment.

It was in this school of interior mortification that Philip peculiarly excelled, and the practice of these virtues was what he most especially pressed on his children.

As to humility, he laid so much stress on it that it was often noticed that, as he walked about the house, he would be repeating to himself, in a sort of low chant: "*Umiltà e staccamento;*"[19] and as St. John was always repeating to his disciples: "Love one another," so Philip may be said to have been always saying to his: "Be humble and lowly." But his own example was more eloquent than any words could have been.

Like the great St. Francis, Philip believed himself to be the greatest sinner in the world; and accordingly, when he

---

[19] Humility and detachment. -Editor.

happened to hear that any one had committed a great sin, he would exclaim: "Thanks be to God that I have not done worse." He would often read the life of St. Mary of Egypt, because, as he said, though he had not imitated her offences against God, he wished to imitate her penance. When he went to confession he was in the habit of saying, while he wept bitterly: "I have never done any good;" and this thought was so present with him at other times, that when he saw young persons he would exclaim: "Oh! happy are you, who have time to do good, a thing which I have never done." Also, when he saw religious, he would break forth with the words: "Oh! happy you, who have left the world, which I should never have had the heart to do." He used to say that his only preparation for saying Mass was to offer himself, so far as depended on himself, to commit every wickedness if God did not help him to do otherwise; and in the same spirit, every day as he held the Blessed Sacrament in his hand, he would say: "Lord, beware of me today, for I shall betray Thee, and commit every possible sin." At other times he would say: "The wound in Jesus' side is large, but if God did not keep His hand upon my head I should make it larger." And when he was about to communicate, he would say with deep emotion: "Lord, I protest before Thee that I am good for nothing except to commit sin." Also, when he was ill, he would say that God had sent him that illness in order to convert him. And once, when Costanzo Tassone wished him to reprove some persons who, though they were under obligations to him, had behaved very badly to him, he only replied: "If I were humble God would not send me such a trial."

Actuated by the same spirit, he was always wont to ascribe to others the merit of whatever there was of good in himself. Though he was such a master of prayer, and before he knew St. Ignatius, he had received from God the miraculous palpitation and the other extraordinary favours which have been mentioned elsewhere, yet, happening one day to meet some Jesuit fathers in the street, he said to them: "You are the sons of a great father; and I, also, am under obligations to him, since it was Ignatius who taught me how to make mental prayer." He would also attribute the favours which God granted him to the prayers of others, or to anything except his own sanctity. Thus, the church having on one occasion been felt to shake while he was saying Mass in the presence of only one old woman and the server, when his Mass was over, the server asked him if he had not felt the trembling like an earthquake? Whereupon he answered: "It was the prayer of that old woman that caused it." And on another occasion, when Baronius spoke to him about a miracle that he had worked, he answered: "Cæsar, you do not know how much pain it gives me to be highly thought of; and I constantly pray God not to work through me things which may lead people to think that I am what I am not. Believe me, if anything supernatural has ever taken place through my instrumentality, it has been owing to the faith of others, and not to any merits of mine."

But that in which his humility shone out with the greatest lustre, was in his conduct towards others. Though he was so much beloved and revered by all around him, he seemed always to consider himself their inferior. Hence, he gave few commands; and when he was obliged to do so, he never spoke in a dictatorial tone, but always as if he owed respect to those whom he was addressing. He was very considerate not to impose too much on those who were subject to him, and not to let any one suffer the least inconvenience on his account. Thus, he used to wear felt slippers when he was in his own room, in order that, as he walked about it, he might not disturb those who occupied the rooms beneath. In his general demeanour and conversation he was always sweet and gentle; and when there were consultations about important matters connected either with himself or others, he was ever ready to take the opinion not only of his superiors, but even of those who, though his inferiors, God gave him light to see had a spirit of true devotion. He had such a dislike to speaking unnecessarily about himself, that he was careful not even to say: "I have said," or "I have done" such or such a thing; and those who were in close society with him remarked, that they had never seen in him the least trace of self-complacency, whence they were of opinion that, like St. Thomas Aquinas, he was exempt from all movements of vainglory.

He wished his penitents, from motives of humility, to avoid all singularity, except where it was specially called for. In forming his congregation he arranged that the mode of living should have nothing singular about it, the beds, the food, and even the dress of the fathers, being the same as were then in common use among secular priests. In this he had himself set them the example; for though he had slept on the bare ground while he was leading his solitary life as a layman, yet from the time he was ordained, he used an ordinary bed with two mattresses, like other persons in the world. From a similar motive he required the fathers to eat whatever was set before them in the refectory, and not to ask for any particular sort of food for themselves; and also in preparing for Mass, he would have them take whatever the sacristan gave them, and not indulge their fancy in the selection of particular vestments or chalices. Even in their devotions he wished his penitents to avoid all singularity, bidding them reserve any demonstration of sensible devotion till they should be alone.

Philip was desirous that the humility of his penitents should have a deeper foundation than mere exterior practices, and he therefore sought to keep constantly before them the great Christian truths, that of themselves they could do nothing good, and that whatever good there might be in them proceeded from God alone. He used often to say to them: "Throw yourselves boldly on God, for if He wishes for anything from you, He will fit you in all things for the work in which He is pleased to use you." He advised them not to ask God for afflictions, but rather to pray Him to give them patience to bear their daily trials. He warned them not to put themselves into the way of temptation, saying, that he feared less for one who, though tempted, is careful to avoid the occasions of sin, than for those who are not tempted, but run headlong into danger. He therefore advised them to say frequently with their whole heart: "Lord, do not trust me, for I shall certainly fall if Thou dost not come to my aid." He also especially recommended them never to say, in times of temptation: "I am resolved not to say or to do" so and so; but rather to say with deep humility: "I know what I ought to do, but I know not whether I shall do it."

He was also in the habit of recommending frequent confession as one of the best ways of obtaining humility; and he advised his penitents to begin by confessing the sins of which they were the most ashamed, as being the best way of confounding the devil. He would not allow them to make excuses for themselves, calling those who did so "Madonna Eva," and telling them that those who wish to be saints, instead of making excuses, ought rather to take blame to themselves for those things of which they are innocent. He used also to tell them that they ought not to be cast down when they were reproved: "for," said he, "the fault which is committed by mourning over the reproof, is often greater than that for which the reproof was given, since this sort of sorrow generally springs from nothing but pride." Hence when they fell, he would have them only humble themselves by some such words as these: "If I had been humble I should not have fallen."

He was also careful to teach them to avoid all that might tempt them to vainglory, as that would be to them not only an occasion of venial sin, but would also endanger the loss of any little humility which they might have acquired. He bade them never to speak, whether in jest or in earnest, in their own praise; saying, that they should not only shun the applause of men, but ask God to hide whatever graces He might be pleased to bestow on them, lest they might prove occasions of vainglory; and that if they had done any good work, and the merit of it was given to another, they ought to rejoice and thank God for it as for a great benefit, since the honour which they lost before men would be restored to them manifold before God. And if perchance any of them told what would redound to his own glory, he would immediately reprove him by saying: *"Secretum meum mihi, secretum meum mihi:"* meaning to intimate that we ought not to publish the secret inspirations or other favours which God may have granted us.

Like the Fathers of the Desert, he used to distinguish three degrees of vainglory; namely, the first, which precedes an action and is the motive for doing it, and which he called the mistress; the second, which arises in the course of an action, but is not the motive for it, and this he called the companion; and the third, which also springs up in the course of an action, but is instantly repressed, and this he called the servant. Whence he was wont to say: "Take care at least that vainglory be not the mistress of your actions; for when it is only their companion it does not rob them of their merit, though perfection consists in making it your servant."

Finally, he used to say that there are four steps in the acquisition of perfect humility, namely: *"Spernere mundum, spernere nullum, spernere se ipsum, spernere se sperni;"* adding, as if in consideration of the great difficulty of attaining these steps, and especially the last: *"et hæc sunt dona superni;"* or at other times: "I have not yet attained to this," or: "I wish I could attain to this."

CHAPTER XIX

 N VIEWING the spiritual training of St. Philip, the most casual observer cannot fail to remark that its two most striking characteristics are, the great freedom which he allowed his children, and the perfect obedience which he required from them. He did not bind them by any vow or promise; he left them the full control of their worldly wealth; he imposed on them no severe, inflexible rule, and burdened them with no compulsory obligations; while, even in the devotions which he introduced, and in the tone of his direction, there breathed a spirit of liberty, so that it has been said that, from his time there may be traced in the teaching of spiritual writers a freer spirit than was to be found in them during the ages which immediately preceded him. And yet at the same time he used to insist that without obedience one cannot make the least progress in perfection; and so skillfully did he lead his children to obey him, that it has been affirmed that their obedience was not inferior to that of the monks of the desert, and that no head of a religious order was ever obeyed so perfectly as he was. He had, indeed, a peculiar art of making the practice of this virtue easy and attractive, while at the same time it was carried to the highest point of perfection. Nay, so beautiful was the union of liberty and obedience which he has left as an heirloom to his children, that the only similitude for it is to be found in that glorious liberty which the saints enjoy in paradise, and which consists in the will being emancipated from sin and concupiscence, and finding its true freedom in union with the will of God.

The complete subjection of the will and understanding, was the ground on which St. Philip based the practice of obedience. He used to say: "that a man's sanctity lies within the space of three inches," at the same time placing his fingers on his forehead, and adding, that the whole matter consists in mortifying the understanding,[20] and in not wishing to act the prudent, and reason too much about everything. He would also say that perfection depends upon making captive one's will, and treating it as if one was lord over it; and that he did not make much account of bodily mortifications, done at a man's own will, but would rather have his penitents conquer their understanding in little things, if they wished to conquer in great things and to make progress in virtue. It was, however, no easy task to lead his children to resign their will so completely as to make his will their own; for, in order to do so, a deep foundation of faith and love was needed on their part, and no little patience, gentleness, and heavenly wisdom on his. He was so conscious of the difficulties attending this part of his work, that he used to say, that no one can conceive how hard it is to keep together those whose obedience is free, and that the only way to accomplish it, is to be very gentle, and to give few commands, so that he who wishes to be well obeyed must order very little. Accordingly he was not in the habit of saying authoritatively: "Do this," or "Do that," but he would rather ask his penitents as a favour to do what he wished, sometimes even adding: "If you find it hard, I will do it," and at other times saying: "I wish to impose such and such a thing on you. What do you say to it?" This forbearance was, however, only a part of that sweet and gentle guile by which he drew on unconsciously those who were not advanced in virtue; while, from those of whose faith and love he was well assured, he would require acts of

---

[20] Mortificar la razionale.

the most extraordinary obedience; and, however extravagant were the things which he ordered, he never failed to be instantly obeyed. So unlimited was the confidence which he inspired, that many of his penitents affirmed that if he had ordered them to jump out of the window, or to throw themselves into the fire, they would instantly have obeyed.

From his own congregation he naturally required more than from others. He left their obedience free from all compulsory obligation, for they might quit the congregation at any moment they liked, without the least sin; but so long as they remained in it, he required from them the most perfect obedience to the few commands which he laid on them. The following is what he wrote on this subject: "If perchance a man knows that he cannot go on without making a disturbance, whether about the table, or the service of the Church, or anything else, let him ask permission, and leave our congregation as quickly as possible; otherwise, after the first or second fault, he will be sent away. For, fathers, I am most determined not to have in the house any one who does not observe the few orders which are given him." He was so strict in requiring them to mortify their will, that if he perceived they had a great repugnance to doing what he ordered, or if they tried to excuse themselves from doing it, he would insist more than ever on being obeyed; and he would often order them to do things at hours and seasons which were contrary to human prudence; because, he said, he was very anxious that his sons should be humble, and not run after wonderful things too high for them. He used to say that, in order to be obedient, it is not enough to do what is ordered, but that it ought to be done without any reasoning about it; and accordingly, when he found that persons argued or made objections to the commands laid on them, he thought slightingly of them, notwithstanding their other good qualities. He was also very particular in requiring them to leave everything, even prayer, for community duties; nor would he allow them to choose their own hour for saying Mass, or to select any particular altar or vestments, but bade them submit themselves in all such matters to the sacristan.

Though he was usually so gentle, yet he would be greatly displeased with those who failed to conform themselves to the rules of the community, as, for instance, if they did not take their place at table with the others, reproving them severely for thus disturbing the general comfort, and adding, that one ought to hold it for certain that what is ordered by those who stand in the place of God, is the best and most perfect, though it may appear quite the contrary.

Though Philip could not claim the same authority over his other penitents, yet he was no less urgent in pressing obedience on them also, saying that all who really wish to make progress in the ways of God ought voluntarily to place themselves under a wise and discreet confessor, whom they should obey entirely and in all things in the place of God, because obedience is the shortest road to perfection, and also the true holocaust which is to be offered up to God on the altar of the heart; so that he who lives an ordinary life under obedience, is to be more highly esteemed than he who, of his own will, performs great penances. He advised persons to think and pray a great deal before they chose a confessor; but after they have chosen him, not to leave him, except for some very good reason, but always to have great faith in him, to lay open to him all their affairs with great simplicity and frankness, and never to undertake anything without his advice, saying, that if they did thus they might be assured that God would never call them to account for their actions, and that He would not allow their confessor to err in anything which concerned their salvation. He used also to say that there is nothing which so completely destroys the snares which the devil lays for us, as following the will of another in our good works; and that, consequently, when the devil cannot lead a person into great sins, he sets himself to excite distrust between him and his confessor, whereby he comes gradually to gain a great deal. Moreover, he wished them to accustom themselves to be obedient even in the most trifling matters, which appear to be of no moment, because in this way a person easily acquires the habit of obedience in greater things.

To those whom he had sent into religion, and who came afterwards to see him, he would say, that if they should happen to be in a place where they were doing a great work for souls, and they received an obedience to go where their success was uncertain, they ought to quit everything willingly, and without making the least objection; for the obedience was a sign that God did not want this fruit through their means. He used also to tell them that it is not enough to see whether God wishes for the good work in which we are engaged, but also whether He wishes for it through us in that way, and at that time, all of which can be discerned only by true obedience. Moreover, he warned them that in order to be perfect, it did not suffice to honour and obey their superiors, but that they must also honour and obey their equals, and even their inferiors.

Confessors, he said, were to blame if, from negligence or human respect, they neglected the opportunities which offered of exercising their penitents in obedience; and he advised them, instead of imposing corporal penances on them, to mortify their will and intellect by obedience, being accustomed to say that the mortification of one passion, however small, does more good than a number of abstinences, fasts, and disciplines.

Philip was greatly aided in this part of his work by the

extraordinary powers with which God had endowed him. One Sunday morning, Baronius having gone rather late to confession, Philip refused to listen to him, and ordered him to go immediately to the hospital of the Santo Spirito. Baronius objected that it was after the usual hour for visiting the hospitals, but Philip only replied: "Go and perform the obedience." Baronius went, and in walking through the hospital, came across a man who was dying; and on questioning him he found, that having been received into the hospital the day before after the usual hours, he had been put to bed without making his confession, and that having since become much worse, he had received extreme unction, but had not made his confession. Baronius accordingly heard his confession, and brought him the Viaticum, immediately after receiving which the poor man expired. On his return, Baronius related what had occurred, when Philip replied: "Go, now, and learn another time to obey without answering."

On another occasion Tarugi having come to confession, Philip said to him: "What news is there of such a person?" naming a very respectable woman, who was a servant in the Hospital of St. James for incurables. "How long is it since you saw her? Go and visit her, and afterwards come to confession, for I feel an interior uneasiness on account of her soul." Tarugi went and found the woman expiring, so that he had arrived just in time to help her through her last agony.

It was universally remarked that those who obeyed Philip, prospered in what they undertook, while misfortune never failed to overtake those who disobeyed him. Vincenzio Crescenzi one day asked and obtained Philip's permission to take a drive with some other young men, and as they were about to set out Philip gave them his blessing. As they were returning Vincenzio fell from the carriage, and one of the wheels went over both his legs, whereupon his companions began to scream, thinking that his legs must be broken; but he jumped up, and went the rest of the way on foot, saying: "Our father's obedience has saved me." On hearing the circumstance, Philip repeated several times: "That was a miracle, and you ought to remember it, and thank God for it."

A young Roman noble declared that he was obliged on his marriage to go a great deal into society; when, if he went with Philip's permission, he was not troubled with bad thoughts, but if he went without it the contrary took place.

Fabrizio dei Massimi's two sons being very ill, he thought of taking them for change of air to a country-seat of his about twenty-eight miles from Rome; but the doctors dissuaded him from it, saying, that if he removed the boys they would certainly die. Philip, however, advised him to go, and bade him begin the journey the next day without the least doubt about it. Fabrizio had more faith in Philip than in the doctors; he took the children into the country, and both of them were immediately restored to health.

On another occasion, however, Fabrizio did not show the same faith in Philip, and he had reason to rue the consequences. He was going to the same country-seat for the summer, and before he went Philip bade him call in some money which he had placed on the life of his daughter Elena; but Elena being young and in good health, Fabrizio saw no occasion for doing so. In the course of the following September Elena fell ill, and died before there was time to recall the money, which was, consequently, lost to her father.

A noble family who were intimate with Philip, being about to make a pecuniary arrangement with a relative, whose heirs they were, but who was in perfect health, Philip said: "Do not make it, for your relative will soon die." The family believed Philip, and obeyed, and their relative dying within a few days, they inherited all his property.

On the other hand, Tarugi having persisted in getting up at night to pray, after Philip had forbidden him to do so, he brought on an attack of the brain, which prevented his praying for eleven months.

Philip once told one of his penitents not to go to Tivoli, and another not to go to Naples, but they both disregarded his advice and went: the one, however, fell from his horse and broke his leg, while the other was nearly lost at sea. Another of his penitents would persist, contrary to his advice, in associating with a certain person, whereupon he said of him: "He will come to a bad end;" and before very long this young man killed his companion in the Campo dei Fiori, and being obliged to fly, was never heard of again.

Philip used to say that penitents ought never to try and overpersuade their confessors to give them leave to do as they wished; and that when they happened not to have full directions from their confessor, they ought to interpret his mind to the best of their power, and then on the first opportunity give him an account of what they had done, so as to avoid any mistake.

From the foregoing instances it may be seen how completely Philip left his penitents free to obey him or not, as they might feel disposed. He once expressed himself on this subject to a young ecclesiastic, who having accepted a prelature contrary to his advice, tried afterwards to extort from him an approval of what he had done. "I give my opinion once and again," said he: "and after that I leave people to do as they like."

The following instances will show that it was no empty boast, when Philip's penitents declared, that if he had ordered them to throw themselves out of the window, or into the fire, they would instantly have obeyed.

On one occasion, as he was walking by a fish-pond with several of his sons, and was exhorting them to the practice of obedience, he chanced to say: "Which of you, now, would be so ready to obey, that if I were to order him to jump into that pond, he would do it?" Scarcely had he spoken the words, than one of them, misunderstanding him, jumped into the water, which was deep enough to have drowned him, but he was rescued by his companions without having received any injury.

On another occasion Philip called Baronius, who had a disorder of the stomach, and bade him eat a piece of bread and a lemon which he offered him. Though the lemon would naturally have been very bad for him, Baronius obeyed, and, as a reward for his faith, he was quite cured. Baronius affirmed that during nine years that he visited the hospital of Santo Spirito in obedience to Philip, it often happened that when he went to the hospital he would be suffering from fever, but after completing his appointed task he would return home in perfect health. Such cases of faith and obedience might be multiplied almost infinitely.

CHAPTER XX

 LOSELY CONNECTED with the virtue of obedience is that of interior mortification, of which Philip was considered to be a perfect master. He valued it far above the greatest corporal penances, and also considered it to be so essential to prayer that he used to say, that for a person to expect to have the spirit of prayer without having first exercised himself in mortification, was as if a bird were to try to fly before it was fledged. He looked on it as the great test of sanctity, far above ecstacies and other extraordinary gifts; so that when persons who were supposed to have attained to a high state of perfection were sent to him in order that he might judge of their spirit, he would begin by subjecting them to mortifications, considering that there could be no great sanctity without a proportionate spirit of mortification.

In imposing mortifications on his penitents Philip acted on his usual principles, selecting them so as to meet their several foibles, and apportioning them to the strength of each, putting to the most severe trials those of whose virtue he was well assured, and dealing more gently with those who were less advanced; so that, notwithstanding his great love of this virtue, some persons remained under his direction for thirty or forty years without receiving a single mortification. So unerring was his judgment, that it was remarked that he never ordered any one to practise a mortification, however extravagant, that he was not obeyed, and that the penitent did not derive great profit from it. In the earlier part of his life he used to impose exterior mortifications, which were most trying from their singularity and publicity, while at the same time they were most useful in raising a man above the fear of public opinion. But in his latter years he gave up doing so, because, when the motive of such actions became known, they lost their effect, and might with many become occasions of pride and vainglory. Many of his mortifications which are commonly related, are, therefore, to be taken not as examples of his general practice, but as illustrations of the unrelenting spirit with which he wished his more advanced penitents to mortify self under every form.

There are few persons who have not some point on which they may be said more or less to pride themselves, which is the touchstone of their honour, and in which self, when driven from all other parts, makes its last secret hiding-place. In frivolous and worldly persons this sort of pride quickly betrays itself, and draws down contempt and ridicule; but in those of better governed minds and higher principles it often takes the form of a virtue, and wins respect by the air of consistency and propriety which it throws round all their actions. The hardest trial, then, to which a man can be put, is to force him to do something which is unworthy of himself, as the phrase goes—something which is unsuitable to his rank and position in society, or to his personal character, whether as a gentleman, or as a man of taste, or of learning, or of high spiritual attainments; and the trial is often the more severe in proportion as his estimate of himself is well founded, and his notions of what is expected from him are correct. It was, however, against this stronghold of pride and human reason that Philip directed his chief mortifications, for he said that no one can advance far in spiritual perfection if he cannot bear the loss of his honour.

His noble penitents, who were naturally prone to think

much of their rank and the claims of society, he would send to beg at the doors of the churches, or to go round from house to house asking for broken pieces of bread; or to make collections during the sermons, which was not then a general custom; or to sweep before the churches and carry away the sweepings. One young man he ordered to walk through the most frequented parts of Rome ringing a bell, the noise of which called the people from the houses, when no cause for the disturbance appearing, they thought him mad, and followed him with hissings and hootings.

Others, whose foible was personal vanity, he mortified on that point. Having noticed that a young man was pleased with a new dress that he wore, he sent him to beg at the door of Santa Maria Maggiore, bidding him eat nothing that day except what he got in alms, and sending after him some of his other penitents to laugh at him. Some of his other penitents he ordered to go to the Minerva, and to lie flat on their faces in the choir during compline till the *Salve Regina* was sung. One of his penitents who was very reluctant to part with the long curls which were then in fashion, he sent to Fra Felice, the Capuchin, to have them cut off, whereupon the monk, who had a hint from Philip, shaved his head.

Sometimes, too, he mortified his penitents by imposing on them foolish or ill-timed actions. He kept by him several pairs of spectacles, which he would put first on one and then on another of the youths who came to visit him, and then set them to do all sorts of work for him. In the same spirit, happening one summer's evening to meet in the passage Marcello Vitelleschi, a shy and sensitive young Roman noble, he took off a habit lined with fur which he had on, and putting it on Marcello with the fur outside, he bade him take a message to Baronius, who was then at vespers in the church. As there were several cardinals and other persons of rank in the choir, Marcello, feeling ashamed to appear before them in this harlequin guise, crept round behind the benches; but this little artifice did not pass unobserved by Philip, who forthwith ordered him to carry the message through the centre of the choir, and Marcello obeyed without hesitation.

On another occasion he went, accompanied by several of his young penitents, to call on Cardinal Alessandrino, and as they were about to take their leave, he said to the Cardinal: "My lord, I wish you would give me something for these sons of mine." The cardinal understood him, and opening a cupboard, took out a large cake and offered it to him, whereupon Philip thanked him, saying: "This is just what I wanted," and took his leave. On getting into the street he divided the cake between the young men, and made them eat it as they walked along, as if they had been a set of unmannerly schoolboys.

Alberto, a carpenter, asked his leave to wear a hair shirt, and Philip consented; but knowing that bodily austerities would cost Alberto much less, and be less useful to him than braving public opinion, he added the condition that the hair shirt should be worn outside of his other clothes. Alberto obeyed, and to his dying day he was never seen in any other dress, so that he got the nickname of Berto of the hair shirt.

Even to those who from their spiritual character seemed entitled to be spared these public mortifications, Philip allowed no exemption. He made Father Bozzio lie for a long time on his face before his confessional, while the people were coming to confession; and he imposed a like penance on a priest who was of a melancholy temper and suffered from scruples. He often had recourse to mortifications to cure scruples, obliging those who suffered from them to publish them openly either in the church or the refectory.

One of his most ingenious yet simple devices for mortifying his penitents, was a dog which had left its master and attached itself to him, continuing faithful to him till its death. He would make his penitents wash and comb it; and, though it was a large dog, he would sometimes make one of them carry it through the street, not even exempting persons of high rank who were generally known; and, at other times, he would make them lead it along by a string, and as the dog ran hither and thither they were dragged after it, to the great diversion of all whom they met. The dog lived with him for fourteen years, during which time it was the instrument of so many and such cruel mortifications to them all, that Tarugi used to call it "the cruel scourge of human minds."

As to the members of the congregation, he never ceased to exercise them in this virtue, sometimes sending them out without the cloak which priests generally wear in Rome, and at others making them wear a baretta of white cloth, or a large antique hat, or a masquerade beard with gold fringe, or go into church with a large rosary like a hermit's round their necks. He made Father Pietro Consolini go about Rome for a long time with a large piece of violet coloured silk fringed with gold round his hat. Sometimes he would send them to the booksellers' shops to ask for books with extravagant titles; and at other times, he would make them wear ragged habits with torn sleeves. On one occasion, a gentleman met one of them in this costume, and believing him to be really poor, he offered him a pair of new sleeves, which the other refused; but Philip, on hearing of it, sent him back to the gentleman, and bade him say that though he had before declined his offer of new sleeves, yet now being in great want of them, he would be very thankful for them.

Philip was also constantly mortifying those who showed any talent for preaching, sometimes ordering them to preach when they least expected it and had made no preparation; and at other times, when they had got interested in their subject and were speaking with great fervour and fluency, he would send one of the others to tell them to stop, because they were saying what was not right, and to bid them sit down, as he himself wished to speak. On one occasion, Father Agostino Manni preached a very beautiful sermon, whereupon Philip ordered him to repeat it six times; so that when he got into the pulpit, people used to smile and say: "Here comes the father who can preach only one sermon." On another occasion, Tarugi having spoken in a sermon about the excellence of suffering, in a way which had a great effect on all who were present, Philip was so much afraid that he might be tempted to vainglory, that he began to strike a pilaster with his hand, so as to attract attention from the preacher to himself; and when Tarugi had finished his sermon, he got up in his place and said, that none of the congregation had any reason to take merit to themselves on the ground of their sufferings, for not one of them had ever shed a single drop of his blood for Christ's sake, but on the contrary had only gained honour and respect by following and serving Him.

He sought especially to mortify those whose noble birth or talents might the more easily betray them into secret pride. On this ground he never ceased to mortify Tarugi. Though Tarugi felt the heat so much that even in winter he could not bear anything warmer than a thin stuff habit, yet Philip made him wear a fur-skin under his habit during three months of the summer. He used sometimes to make him sing comic songs in the presence of cardinals and nuns, and other grave personages, and at others he would send him to carry loads to different places, or make him stand in the middle of the refectory and ask for his meals as an alms for the love of God. He used also to mortify him when he was a layman, by keeping him without Holy Communion for six or eight months; and after he was a priest, because his fervour made him shed tears during his Mass, he would not allow him to celebrate more than three times, and afterwards five times a week. Besides all these petty mortifications, he pretended on one occasion to be very angry with him, and, without assigning any reason, ordered him to quit the congregation. Tarugi was heartbroken at this unexpected blow, and ceased not to weep night and day, and to make the most diligent examination of all his actions, in hopes of discovering his fault. At last he sent Father Bozzio to intercede for him, he himself remaining outside the door of Philip's room. Philip seemed to be mollified by Bozzio's entreaties, but in order to show that he knew by an interior light that Tarugi was at the door, he ordered him to come in; when, after Tarugi had thrown himself at his feet and made the most humble apologies, he received him back into his favour, bidding him, however, take care never again to do anything which would make him unworthy to live in that house. Philip afterwards told Father Bozzio, that he could not conceive how much merit Tarugi had gained while he had been thus severely mortified.

Baronius also underwent a more than common share of mortification. It has already been told how, in order to keep him humble in the midst of his literary pursuits, Philip would allow him no exemption from the performance of his ordinary duties. Besides these daily trials, he used at one time to send him constantly to buy a very small quantity of wine, bidding him take a very large flask to fetch it in, and laying on him strict injunctions to make the people in the wine-shop wash out the flask carefully before they put the wine in, and to go with them into the cellar to see them draw it, while at the same time he would give him a large gold coin, which he was to offer in payment of the few pence which the wine would cost. The consequence was, that the wine-vendors would get so angry with Baronius for making such a fuss, and giving so much trouble about such a paltry purchase, that they would load him with abuse, and would even threaten to give him a good thrashing. Poor Baronius would sometimes feel inclined to rebel, and he would often wonder how Philip could be so inconsiderate and so fussy about such a trifle; for Philip always gave his orders in such a simple, natural way, that Baronius never dreamt of suspecting that the whole was premeditated in order to mortify him. On one occasion, however, Philip carried his mortification so far that Baronius rebelled, feeling certain that he had right on his side; but this was the very reason why Philip had selected this opportunity for trying him, and why he insisted on being obeyed.

As Baronius had been discarded by his family, and had nothing of his own, he could not contribute the usual sum towards the expenses of the congregation, and was, therefore, excused from doing so. It happened, however, that after some time the Pope gave him a small pension, in order to enable him to get manuscripts copied, and to meet the other expenses attending his great work; and as Baronius could not now plead poverty, Philip called upon him, in obedience to a rule of the congregation, to pay the usual sum. Baronius, however, took another view of the case, and looking on the pension as given for a specific purpose, hesitated to obey, and used many sound arguments to bring Philip round to his opinion. At last he sent Father Tommaso Bozzio to try what he could do; but Philip remained inexorable, and even told Bozzio that if Baronius would not contribute, he must quit the congregation. Bozzio accordingly turned his efforts to persuading Baronius to submit; and at last Baronius, being induced to follow his good advice, went to Philip's room, and humbly begging pardon for his obstinacy, placed at his disposal not only his little pension, but himself and all that he might ever possess.

This was all that Philip wanted, and he therefore replied: "Now you have done what you ought. That is enough; for I want nothing from you. Only learn another time to obey promptly."

CHAPTER XXI

HERE was one other virtue to which Philip attached great weight as a means of attaining perfection, and that was perseverance. He had constantly on his lips our Lord's words: "He that shall endure to the end, he shall be saved;" and remembering that each man's final sentence for eternity will depend on his perseverance, he made that virtue his own test of perfection, estimating actions and practices of devotion, not according to what seemed to be great and heroic in them, but according to the steadiness with which they were persevered in. For the same reason he appointed five Paters and Aves to be said every evening in the Oratory for the grace of perseverance.

Perseverance may be seen at a glance to have been one of the chief characteristics of Philip's own life. From the time that he first came to Rome, he never went beyond its walls, except so far as was necessary for the purpose of making the pilgrimage to the Seven Churches; and, though his friends would often urge him to go with them to different places, and especially to Florence, he could never be prevailed on to do so, answering, in reference to a proposal for visiting his native place: "that he had no country except heaven." Also, from the time he became a priest and confessor, he devoted himself exclusively to the duties of these two offices, so that his life may be said to have been spent in praying, preaching, administering the sacraments, and visiting the sick. The same spirit directed him in the establishment of the congregation; for, in order to enable the fathers to attend the better to the end of its institution, he would not multiply their occupations, but was content, as he himself said, with assigning them only three duties; namely, prayer, the ministration of the sacraments, and the word of God.

He used to say that he could make any one devout in a short time, but the main thing was to see whether they persevered; and he would laugh when persons, who had gained a little fervour, began to think that they were making great progress, saying, that perfection cannot be attained without great labour, and that one must not expect to do everything in one day, nor to become a saint in four. Also, when he was told of young people who seemed to be making great progress in spiritual things, he would answer: "Wait till they are fledged, and then we shall see how they will fly."

The three things which, he said, tended most to perseverance, were discretion, regularity in the performance of one's ordinary devotions, and great confidence in God. As to discretion he used to say, that he found it more difficult to teach moderation to those who would do too much than to stir up those who did too little; and he would warn such persons to beware of becoming so attached to the means as to forget the end.

As to regularity in their devotions, he enjoined his penitents to see that each day had something to show, often saying to them: "*Nulla dies sine linea.*"[21] He considered devotion to our Lady, and hearing Mass daily, to be great aids to perseverance; and he recommended his penitents not to be easily induced to neglect their daily Mass, nor their confessions on the appointed days; saying, that they should first hear Mass or make their confession, and afterwards do whatever they had thought of substituting for these duties.

---

[21] "No day without a line." In Latin linea may mean a string, and in the usage of St. Philip's day the string would refer to a rosary. -Editor.

He advised them to undertake only a few prayers, and to say these regularly and devoutly rather than overload themselves with a great number of devotions, of which they would soon become weary, when they would either give them up entirely or perform them carelessly; adding, that if the devil can persuade us to neglect our accustomed exercises only once, it will be easier for him to do so a second time, and still easier on a third occasion, till at last all our good practices will end in nothing. On this account he wished them to be very particular to avoid little acts of negligence, and to correct all their little faults; and he recommended them constantly to renew any good resolutions which they might once have made, and not to heed any temptations to abandon them.

Finally, as to confidence in God, he used to say, that they should never forget that God is always the same as He has ever been, and that therefore they should not be discouraged by the changes in their spiritual state; for God is accustomed to give great sensible devotion and fervour to beginners, and after a time: "He makes as though He would go farther," in order to try them, often allowing them to be greatly troubled by temptations to some vice, as a means of leading them on to the practice of the opposite virtue which He designs to confer on them. He advised them, therefore, on such occasions, not to be disturbed, but to keep up their courage by recalling the favours which they had formerly enjoyed, being assured that if they fought bravely and conquered their present temptations, God would eventually give them spiritual consolations far surpassing those which they had had in past times.

Philip used to divide the spiritual life into three degrees; namely, the animal, the human, and the angelic. The animal life, he said, is that of those who run after sensible devotion; the human life, that of those who experience no sensible devotion, but combat their passions, and strive after virtue, this being the peculiar obligation of human beings; while the angelic life is that of those, who, after a long struggle, have conquered their passions, and have received from God the grace to lead, even in this world, a quiet and peaceful life like that of the angels, without being troubled or afflicted by anything whatsoever. He recommended his penitents to be careful to persevere in the second till such time as it should please God to grant them the third.

He was very averse to every kind of change, and wished all his penitents, whether religions or laymen, to remain in the state in which God had called them; telling religious who wished to leave their order because the discipline was relaxed, that they ought to remain where they were, as it might be God's will to use them for the reformation of the order; and bidding laymen follow their ordinary callings, since "in the midst of a crowd one may practise perfection, and no trade or occupation need be an impediment to the service of God." Persons who lived at court, and gave great edification to those around them, he would not easily permit to quit their position for one of a spiritual character, saying: "that it requires no deliberation to pass from a bad state to a good one, but it needs much time, counsel, and prayer, before passing from a good one to a better; for the devil often transfigures himself into an angel of light, and tempts us to give up the good state under the false pretence of leading us to a better one."

Though Philip sent so many persons into religion, and was anxious to do so whenever he saw a decided vocation; yet, in general, he preferred persons remaining where they were, and made great difficulties to their entering religion, saying, that "though the religious state is the highest, it does not suit every one," often keeping his penitents back for months and even for years, and subjecting them to the severest mortifications before he would give his consent. By this means he tested their perseverance, so that many of those whom he sent into convents would say, when they afterwards came to see him, that if he had not subjected them to these trials, they would never have had the virtue to persevere in their religious life. The only cases in which he acted differently were those in which a person avoided an occasion of sin by going into religion, and then he would advise him at once to take the step.

He made the same difficulty about allowing persons to quit their position, because it did not seem to suit them, or because they found its duties too burdensome. One of his penitents, Maximilian Borgo, had unwillingly accepted a situation in the service of a nobleman, stipulating, however, that he should not be employed in any secular matters, in order that he might have the more leisure for his religious exercises and the service of God. The nobleman was not very careful to observe the contract, whereupon Maximilian wished to resign his post, and consulted Philip on the subject; but Philip advised him to be patient and remain where he was, telling him plainly that: "if he fled from this cross, he would find a greater elsewhere, and would never again be settled." Notwithstanding, Maximilian could not make up his mind to follow Philip's advice, but quitted the nobleman's service. In the end, however, he had reason to lament the decision, for Philip's words came true, and though he always continued to lead a good life, yet from this time he never was quiet, but was always changing about from place to place.

CHAPTER XXII

ACH RELIGIOUS BODY in the Church has its own distinctive characteristic, and prayer may be said to be that of St. Philip and his children, as, indeed, is plainly declared by their name of Congregation of the Oratory. The practice and promotion of prayer is their chief obligation; all their occupations are made subservient to this great object; and prayer is the great means to which they look for their own sanctification and that of others, and which supplies to them the want of the detailed instructions and systematic rules, which other religious bodies have received from their several founders.

Philip made so much account of prayer that he used to say, that a man who does not pray is like an animal without reason. And when, during one of his attacks of illness, the doctors forbade him to pray, though he made every effort to obey them, yet he felt that he could not live without prayer, and at last he exclaimed to Father Antonio Gallonio: "Alas! Antonio, it seems to me that I am become a beast." He used to say that there is nothing which the devil fears, and which he tries to hinder so much as prayer; and, accordingly, he would not admit any excuse for neglecting prayer, insisting that no kind or amount of occupation ought to be an interruption to it, and that no temptations or delusions ought to induce us to intermit our accustomed devotions. He exhorted persons to persevere in prayer, even though God might long delay to grant their petition, saying, that when God wills it: "He can do more in one moment of time than in tens of years;" and who can tell but that he may be giving up prayer at the very moment when God is preparing to answer it. He also advised them not to cease praying as soon as God began to answer their prayers, but to persevere till they had obtained the full accomplishment of their wishes; as, for instance, when a person was ill, they should not give up praying as soon as he began to amend, but should continue to pray till he was quite recovered; for as the first improvement had been obtained through prayer, so his final recovery should be looked for through the same means.

Philip did not restrict his penitents to any particular kind of prayer, but rather directed them to trust to the teaching of the Holy Spirit. He used to say that the best way to learn to pray, is to feel one's-self unworthy of such a great benefit, and to throw one's-self entirely into the arms of our Lord, who Himself will teach us to pray. On one occasion, when a penitent asked him to teach him to pray he answered: "Be humble and obedient, and the Holy Spirit will teach you." He said also that persons ought in their prayers to obey the Holy Spirit's guidance; as, for instance, if they were drawn to meditate on the Passion, they ought not to go to something else; and he recommended them when they went to communion, to follow out the subject to which they had been led in their meditations. He recommended beginners to read the lives of the saints, and other spiritual books, saying in his own quaint way, that whether for spiritual reading or as an assistance in prayer, there were no authors to be compared to those whose names begin with St., such as St. Augustine, St. Gregory, St. Bernard, and the other saints. His own favourite books were St. Paul's Epistles, the works of John Gerson, the Quiver of Divine Love, the Lives of St. Catherine of Sienna and Blessed John Colombini, Lipoman's Lives of the Saints, and the Lives of the Fathers of the Desert, of which last he used to read a chapter almost daily. He said, moreover, that such books ought not to be read hurriedly or for curiosity, but slowly, and a little at a time, pausing whenever any devotional feeling is excited, and that great discretion should be used in such reading, and also in the practice of mental prayer, for that, many persons when they once begin to read or pray, do not know when to stop and thereby injure their constitutions, and impair their future happiness. He also advised beginners to meditate frequently on the four last things, often saying: "That he who does not go into hell during his lifetime, runs a great risk of going there after his death."

He was very fond of ejaculatory prayer, because it does not fatigue the mind like lengthened meditation, but may be resumed at all times and in the midst of the greatest distractions. The following are some of the ejaculatory prayers, which he was himself in the constant habit of using:

LATIN EJACULATIONS

Cor mundum crea in me, Deus, et spiritum rectum innova in visceribus meis.

Deus, in adjutorium meum intende: Domino ad adjuvandum me festina.

Doce me facere voluntatem tuam.

Domine, ne te abscondas mihi.

Domine, vim patior, responde pro me.

Ego sum via, veritas, et vita, dixit Dominus.

Fiat voluntas tua sicut in cælo et in terra.

Jesu, sis mihi Jesu; ego non te diligo.

Adauge mihi fidem, O bone Jesu.

Omnis vallis implebitur, et omnis mons et collis humiliabitur.

Verbum caro factum est.

Ne nos inducas in tentationem.

Ne reminiscaris, Domine, iniquitatum mearum.

Quando te diligam filiali amore?

Sancta Trinitas, unus Deus, miserere nobis.

Tui amoris in me ignem accende.

Maria, mater gratiæ, mater misericordiæ, tu nos ab hoste protege, et hora mortis suscipe.

Assumpta Maria in cælum, gaudent Angeli.

VERNACULAR EJACULATIONS

I know Thee not yet, my Jesus, because I do not seek Thee.

My Jesus, what shall I do if Thou dost not aid me?

My Jesus, what can I do to please Thee?

My Jesus, what can I do to fulfil Thy will?

My Jesus, give me the grace not to serve Thee for fear, but for love.

My Jesus, I would fain love Thee.

I distrust myself, but I trust Thee, my Jesus.

My Jesus, I can do no good without Thy help.

My Jesus, I wish to do nothing but Thy most holy will.

My Jesus, I have never loved Thee yet, but I would fain love Thee now.

I shall never love Thee if Thou dost not help me, my Jesus.

I would fain love Thee, my Jesus, but I do not know how.

I seek Thee and do not find Thee, my Jesus.

My Jesus, if I did but know Thee, Thou wouldst know me.

If I should do all the good that is done in the world, what would it be worth after all, O my Jesus?

I shall fall, my Jesus, unless Thou upholdest me. My Jesus, if Thou wishest for me, clear away all the hindrances which keep me from Thee.

My Lord, I wish to learn the road to heaven.

My Jesus, without Thy help I know not what to say or

do.

My Jesus, if Thou dost not help me I am ruined. O my Jesus, grant that I may never offend Thee.

O my Blessed Lady, give me grace always to be thinking of thy virginity.

O my Blessed Lady, give me grace always to be calling thee to mind.

Philip was in the habit of teaching his penitents to repeat any one of the above ejaculations sixty-three times, in the form of a rosary in honour of the sixty-three years of our Lady's life; and he also taught them to repeat in the same way, with the Pater, two prayers in our Lady's honour which were always on his own lips, one of which was: "Virgin Mary, Mother of God, pray to Jesus for me," or "pray to thy Son Jesus for me;" while the second was simply: "Virgin Mother!" He also taught a poor woman and her family to repeat the *Pater* and *Ave* forty-nine times every day from Holy Saturday to Whit Sunday as a devotion to the Holy Spirit, telling her that this was an excellent method of obtaining favours from God. The same poor woman related with what patience he had taught her to make mental prayer, by making her meditate on each word of the *Pater* as she repeated it.

But since, as St. Bernard says, our Lady is the neck through which all spiritual blessings descend from Christ the head, devotion to her was what Philip most strongly pressed on all his children. His own affection for her was at once so fervent and so tender, that her name was always on his lips, calling her his love and his consolation, invoking her as the dispenser of all the graces which God graciously grants to the children of Adam, and often addressing her with childlike familiarity as *"Mamma mia."* When he was passing the images of our Lady which are commonly to be found in the streets and squares of Italian towns, he would stop before them for a considerable time to give vent to the affectionate emotions, which the mere sight of them awakened within him. He said that by praying before her image, he had frequently got rid of temptations with which the devil was pursuing him; and when his penitents were troubled by doubts or other evil thoughts, he would recommend them to invoke her aid, and especially to use the above rosaries in her honour. He sometimes spent the whole night in colloquies with her. Father Giovanni Antonio Lucci related, that on one occasion when Philip was ill, and he had to sit up with him through the night, he was afraid he should not be able to remain long with him because the weather was very warm and his room was so small. But it happened that Philip supposed himself to be left alone, and as soon as he thought no one was within hearing, he began to pour out his soul to our Lady in the most tender and impassioned terms, continuing through the livelong night to speak to her as if she were indeed present and he was conversing with her face to face; and Father Antonio Lucci experienced such consolation in listening merely to this sweet colloquy, that when the morning Angelus sounded he thought it was that of the preceding evening, so rapidly had the night passed away.

The following precepts, taken chiefly from St. Bernard and other old writers, were so constantly on Philip's lips that they may be taken to express his own opinions.

He bade his penitents always have high aspirations in prayer, and wish, if possible, to surpass St. Peter and St. Paul in sanctity; for though they would never attain to this point, yet it is well to do at least in will what one cannot accomplish in deed. He reminded them that they must never be satisfied with any degree of perfection to which they might have attained, since our Lord had set before them the perfection of the Eternal Father as the standard at which they should aim, saying to them: "Be you therefore perfect, as also your Heavenly Father is perfect."

He bade them never ask for anything except conditionally; and he advised them when they were in trouble not to be satisfied with their own prayers, but to ask for those of others, as was his own custom, telling them that when they experienced great peace and consolation in asking a favour of God, they might take it as a sign that He either had already granted their request, or would shortly do so.

He used to say that in times of spiritual dryness the best remedy is to imagine ourselves beggars in the presence of God and the saints, and as such to beg first one saint and then another to ask a spiritual alms for us, with the same earnestness with which beggars are wont to ask for temporal relief; and he exhorted his penitents at these times to go from church to church and altar to altar, in order the more earnestly to solicit the intercession of the saints to whom they are severally dedicated. For his own part he always preferred those churches which were the least frequented, and in which there was least chance of distraction.

Philip's efforts to lead his penitents to pray were so successful, that not only priests and religious, but secular persons of all classes, attained under his direction to such perfection in prayer, that they were enabled, amid the turmoil of the world, to lead lives as pure and recollected as if they had been hidden in the desert or the cloister. Many persons, too, were in the habit of assembling their families and servants every evening at the hour at which the meetings were held in the Oratory, and following with them the same devotions which St. Philip had established. Some of them also introduced, as far as was possible, the same kind of community life into their households. In fact, it may be said, in the words of Father Agostino Manni: "that his congregation was given the name of the Oratory, in order to show that he who does not pray cannot belong to it," nor be a child of St. Philip.

The Blessed Virgin appears to St. Philip
-Giovanni Battista Piazzetta

St. Pius V and the Vision of Lepanto

CHAPTER XXIII

 OR SOME YEARS after the establishment of the community at St. Giovanni dei Fiorentini things went smoothly with Philip. He had, of course, the same petty trials as before; worldly people continued to speak ill of him; great men often treated him with contempt; and from time to time some of his penitents went astray, and caused him anxiety and grief. But still God's blessing rested visibly on his work, and his influence throughout Rome increased from day to day. This state of things could not, however, be expected to last for ever. At length, A.D. 1570, there burst on him a storm, at a time and under circumstances which made it peculiarly trying to him.

St. Pius V then filled the papal throne, and his saintly character seemed to guarantee Philip from all opposition in the work to which God had appointed him; and yet it was from him that Philip's trial came. The two last Popes, Paul IV and Pius IV, had regarded him with such veneration, that his enemies had been forced to be silent; but when Pius V, to whom Philip was personally unknown, mounted the papal throne, they once more raised their heads. They accordingly laid before St. Pius an accusation against the exercises at St. Girolamo, complaining that persons not in holy orders, were allowed to expound doctrine and narrate doubtful facts without due explanation, that theological questions were proposed for discussion among ignorant and unlettered persons; that consequently, many foolish and erroneous opinions were advanced without proper pains being taken to correct them, and that thus great scandal was given, and great danger of heresy was incurred by those who were in the habit of attending these meetings. Philip's calumniators were not mistaken in supposing that such a charge as this would meet with attention from St. Pius; for he at once took alarm, and the accusation being well supported, he was at first inclined to believe it. But saints never act hastily; and, therefore, before St. Pius took any decided step, he gave himself time to ascertain the will of God. He sent privately, however, for two Dominican priests, Fra Alessandro Franceschi and Fra Paolino Bernardini, both of them men of great piety and learning, and he commissioned them, unknown to each other, to attend the meetings at St. Girolamo, and report to him whether they heard anything contrary to the faith or to morality.

St. Pius took his measures with so much prudence and charity, that no one except the two Dominican Fathers knew what was going on; and Philip's penitents continued peacefully to follow from day to day their usual devotions, without the least suspicion that their much-loved oratory was in danger. So quiet was the whole matter kept, that if Philip had not been a saint, the storm might have blown over without his ever knowing anything about it. But God intended all this to be an exercise of his faith and patience, and therefore He revealed to him what the Pope was doing.

It must have been a great trial to one who had such a low opinion of himself as Philip, to be suspected by a saint like St. Pius; and at first sight it did indeed look as if there must be something in the oratory exercises which was displeasing to God, and which He had appointed this holy Pope to correct. Besides, nothing is more trying than to have every word secretly listened to, and caught up, and repeated, perhaps in a different sense from that in which it was uttered, and in such cases misinterpretations may easily, and even unconsciously, be given to the most innocent expressions. Moreover, Philip was confined to his room by illness; and, as there was no one to supply his place in the Oratory, it was by no means improbable, that in his absence things might be said, and might pass without notice, which he would have corrected if he had been present; and thus an unfair opinion might readily be formed of their usual proceedings. Still, in spite of these trying circumstances, Philip was silent, and preserved his peace of mind. He had recourse to prayer, and comforted himself, as on a former occasion, with the thought that, as he had begun the exercises purely for God's glory, the same motive would make him willing, at any moment, to give them up; and thus, resting all his hope and confidence in God, he calmly awaited the issue of the Pope's searching inquiry.

It happened that at this time Alessandro de' Medici, afterwards Leo XI, was at Rome as ambassador from the Grand Duke of Tuscany; and, having gone one day to a private audience with the Pope, the latter, who knew that he was acquainted with Philip, mentioned to him the reports that had reached him about the oratory meetings, and particularized several things which, he was told, had been incautiously expressed, especially the story of St. Apollonia, which was reported to have been narrated, without any explanation that she had thrown herself into the fire in obedience to a special inspiration of the Holy Spirit. The Pope finally asked Alessandro to go to the sermons at St. Girolamo, and to let him know what he thought of them. As soon as the audience was over, Alessandro went to the Minerva, where he met Germanico Fedell, who gave him a message from Philip, begging him to come to him at St. Girolamo, because he wished particularly to speak to him, and, being confined to his bed, he could not call on him as he would otherwise have done. Accordingly Alessandro went in the afternoon to St. Girolamo, but, before going up to Philip's room, he went into the Oratory to listen more particularly to the sermons, as the Pope had bid him do. There, to his great surprise, he heard this story of St. Apollonia narrated, and then all the other subjects which the Pope had mentioned were successively touched upon, the whole being done with perfect correctness, and every necessary caution. It was a strange coincidence certainly, though it might, after all, be only accidental; but when Alessandro went to Philip's room, all doubt on this point was speedily removed; for Philip accosted him with the words: "Pray tell me, Signor Alessandro, what the Pope said to you this morning about us?" Alessandro was not a little astonished at this question, for no one had been present when the Pope had spoken to him, and therefore Philip could not have come by his knowledge of their conversation except by Divine revelation; but seeing that he was discovered, he frankly avowed the whole. From this time forth Alessandro looked upon Philip as a saint, and when he afterwards became, first a cardinal, and then Pope, he lost no opportunity of advancing the interests of the congregation.

Meanwhile the two Dominican fathers carried their separate reports to the Pope, when both of them assured him that, so far from having heard anything contrary to sound doctrine or morality, they only wondered at the rare union of fervour, devotion, and prudence which characterized the proceedings. The Pope expressed great pleasure on hearing this, and said how happy he was to think that there should be in Rome a man like Philip, who was so constantly watching and labouring to keep alive a spirit of devotion in those around him. The Dominican fathers were so impressed with all that they had heard, that from this time they went almost daily to the sermons, and often took their turn with the fathers in preaching.

Thus this storm blew over, and what Philip's enemies

had devised for his ruin, was overruled by God for the furtherance of his work. All that had passed was soon known through Rome, and served to draw a great many persons to St. Girolamo; while, henceforth, no one dared to speak publicly against Philip or his exercises.

CHAPTER XXIV

IXTEEN YEARS had now elapsed since Philip had begun the exercises at St. Girolamo, and ten since he had founded the congregation at St. Giovanni; and during all this time, he had never dreamt of doing more than providing from day to day, as an orderly secular priest, for the spiritual wants of the souls which had fallen to his charge. The time, however, was at last come, when the work in which he had been so long engaged, was to assume the permanent form which God had predestined for it. Several concurring circumstances combined to bring this about, so that in this, as in all the other steps of his life, Philip was led on by the providence of God, without any direct exercise of his own will.

Up to the year 1574, the spiritual exercises were held at St. Girolamo, while the community was formed at St. Giovanni, so that the only connection between them was the accidental one that both were under Philip's guidance, and that the principal preachers at St. Girolamo were members of the community at St. Giovanni. In the year 1574 they came to be united, in compliance with the wishes of the Florentines, to whom the church of St. Giovanni belonged. The fathers who lived at St. Giovanni were in the habit of going three times every day, and in all weathers, to St. Girolamo; and as this was a great inconvenience and fatigue to them, the Florentines earnestly entreated Philip to remove the exercises to St. Giovanni, and offered to build a large oratory for the purpose. Philip consented, and the oratory being completed, it was opened on the 15th April, A.D. 1574, from which day the meetings were held there instead of at St. Girolamo.

Still, however, the existence of the Oratory was precarious, as it depended on the life of Philip, who was getting old. If he were to die, the church of St. Giovanni would fall into other hands, the community would be broken up, the fathers would probably be dispersed, the spiritual exercises would be discontinued, and the whole work would come to an end. The fathers had become so attached to the happy fraternal union in which they lived, that they could not bear this sad prospect, and they often entreated Philip to make some future provision for his children. It was very long before he would listen to them, for he could not suppose that God had destined such a lowly individual as himself to carry out any permanent work in the Church; but at last a circumstance occurred, which proved to him the reasonableness of their request.

Among those who had joined the community there was a young man, whom Philip was obliged to send away on account of his ungovernable temper. In revenge, this young man set to work to get Philip turned out of St. Giovanni, and he gave so plausible a colouring to the calumnies he invented, that more than once the Florentines had almost made up their minds to take the church from him. The misunderstanding was soon removed; but it was the means of leading Philip to see that it was the will of God that he should place his community on a more solid foundation; and accordingly, overcoming his humility, he listened to the entreaties of his sons, and consented to their looking out for some place which might be their own, and in which he might, with the Pope's authority, found a permanent congregation.

The two churches which seemed to be most eligible were St. Maria in Monticelli, which could be obtained without difficulty, and St. Maria in Vallicella, then a parish church, the position of which being more central, seemed to be preferable on that account. Philip referred the decision to the Pope, Gregory XIII, who pronounced in favour of St. Maria in Vallicella, and the incumbent being easily induced to resign it on condition that he should retain the income during his lifetime, the fathers took possession of it. Soon after, his Holiness issued a bull, dated 15th July, A.D. 1575, founding the new congregation as a congregation of secular priests, under the name of the Congregation of the Oratory, with all the privileges usually conferred on religious bodies.

As soon as the congregation was founded, and possession had been obtained of their new church, Philip sent Giovan Antonio Lucci and Germanico Fedeli to take charge of the parish which was attached to the latter, and to superintend a few alterations which were necessary for the reception of the community. The fathers did not at first contemplate making any great additions to the church; but when they came to look more closely at it, they found that it was in such a ruinous state, that their best plan would be to pull it down and erect a new one. The only difficulty was, that they had no funds for such a work. One morning, however, they received an order from Philip to pull down the old church and begin at once to build a new one, large and commodious enough for the purposes of the congregation. This was a bold step to take, but they had such confidence in their father, that they did not hesitate to obey. The old church was pulled down, Matteo Castello, the best architect in Rome, was engaged to build the new one, and every arrangement was made for beginning the work; for though no money to meet the expense had yet been found, Philip bade them trust in God, saying: "I know God will help me," and his words inspired them with a similar confidence.

The ground being cleared, Castello came to draw out the foundations with his line; but just as he was about to begin, a message arrived from St. Girolamo, bidding him wait till Philip had said Mass, as he wished to be present at the drawing out of the foundations. Castello accordingly waited, and Philip, as soon as he had finished his Mass, came to the Vallicella. Castello then placed the line at the spot which he thought would make the church sufficiently large, but Philip bade him draw it out further. Castello obeyed, and after drawing the line out a considerable distance, he stopped; but Philip once more said: "Draw it out further." Castello again obeyed; but when he again stopped, Philip said for the third time: "Draw it out further still." So Castello drew on his line till he reached the spot which God had shown in spirit to Philip, and then Philip called out: "Stop, and dig there." They obeyed, and when they had dug down to the depth of ten palms, they came to an old wall, the existence of which was unknown, which served as a support for the foundations on one side of the church, besides furnishing materials for all the foundations, and a great part of the walls.

The first stone of the new church was laid, with the usual solemnities, on the 17th September, A.D. 1575, by Alessandro de' Medici, then archbishop of Florence, and from that time the work proceeded without interruption. The first money was given by St. Charles Borromeo, who sent two hundred crowns; the Pope then gave eight thousand; and after that, large sums were contributed by various persons at different times, so that, when the building was completed, Philip was enabled to say: "that though he had begun to build without any money, yet, by the grace of God, above a hundred thousand crowns had been spent to His honour in the erection of the church." This money, however, came in gradually, as if to try Philip's confidence, and prove that it was God alone who provided for the work.

Sometimes the funds would run very low, and there would be no prospect of their being replenished; and then some persons would almost reproach him for having begun to build on so large a scale; but on such occasions he would only answer: "I have such trust in God, that I should not be afraid to pull down all that has been already built, and to begin another church on a larger and more expensive scale." The result proved that his confidence was not unfounded, for the money came in whenever it was wanted, so that those who saw how much he was always spending, considered that it was miraculously provided. One of the most remarkable circumstances was, that he never asked any one for money, and never allowed any of the congregation to do so. One of the brothers having on one occasion told him that the work must soon come to a stand, because there was no money to continue it, he answered: "Do not fear, for our Lord will provide what is necessary." The brother then suggested that there was a certain gentleman who was very rich, and gave away large sums for the love of God, and that if they asked him, he would probably give them an alms. But Philip replied: "My son, I have never asked for anything, and God has always provided for me. That gentleman knows perfectly well what are our wants, and if he chooses, he can give us an alms without being asked for it." This trustful answer met its reward, for before very long, a lawyer died and left four thousand crowns for the building of the church, and six months after, another person bequeathed above eight thousand for the same purpose.

Philip considered it no trifling subject for congratulation that he should have been led, without any premeditated design, to place his congregation in a church dedicated to our Lady; and during the erection of the new building, our Lady showed in a remarkable manner, that she took it under her special protection. When the old church was pulled down, Father Giovanni Antonio Lucci who superintended the work, thought it desirable to leave standing a small chapel in which he might continue to say Mass and minister the sacraments; but one morning, in the course of the year 1576, Philip sent for him and said: "Go and have the roof of that chapel taken down immediately; for last night I saw that it was falling, and that it was supported only by our Lady, who had placed her hands under it, and was holding it up." Father Lucci instantly obeyed, and when the workmen came to remove the roof, they found that the end of the principal beam on which it rested, had slipped out of the wall, and was hanging suspended in the air, without any support.

The work proceeded rapidly through the year 1576; in due time the building was roofed in, and at the opening of the year 1577, it was so far advanced, that the fathers looked joyfully forward to opening the church in the month of February. But at the moment when their long-cherished hopes seemed about to be accomplished, a dreadful and sudden blow fell on them. Philip was taken dangerously ill, and his fever rose to such a height, that the physicians gave no hopes of his life, and his children almost looked on him as one already dead. He continued, as usual, to communicate daily, and he did so with such fervour, and such an abundance of tears, that his devotion wore out the little strength which still remained to him. It often happened that he lay awake the whole night watching for the happy moment when his Lord should be brought to him; and so intense was the eagerness of his loving expectation, that on one occasion, when Father Antonio Gallonio was rather slow in communicating him, being unable to endure the suspense, he exclaimed: "Antonio, you are holding my Lord in your hand, and you do not give Him to me. Why is this?

Give Him to me, give Him to me."

It happened one night when he was at the worst, that he had not slept at all, but just as the bells began to ring for matins, he desired Tarugi to bring him Holy Communion. Tarugi, however, delayed to obey, because he knew that Philip had not yet had any sleep, and he feared that his devotion after Communion might prevent his getting any rest before morning: but Philip guessing his motive, sent for him and said: "Francesco Maria, I cannot sleep on account of my great desire for the Blessed Sacrament, and I shall not sleep till I have received Him whom I long for. Bring me Holy Communion, for as soon as I have received it, I shall fall asleep." Tarugi could no longer hesitate to obey; and, wonderful to relate, as soon as Philip had communicated, he fell asleep; and when he awoke, his disease was found to have taken a turn, so that he was out of danger. From this time the fathers, seeing that the Blessed Sacrament was his best medicine, brought it to him every morning, and before very long he was restored to his usual health.

Meanwhile, the building had been advancing, and by the middle of February the church was ready to be opened. The first Mass was celebrated in it with great pomp and festivity, by Alessandro de' Medici, archbishop of Florence, on Septuagesima Sunday, the 23rd February, A.D. 1577. In the course of the following April the fathers removed thither, and the spiritual exercises were transferred from St. Giovanni dei Fiorentini to the Chiesa Nuova, as it is generally called. Some years after, on the 11th February, A.D. 1590, the newly-discovered bodies of the Martyrs, St. Papias and St. Maurus, were translated thither, and were deposited under the high altar.

Great crowds were present at the opening of the church, and after the services were commenced, and the exercises were regularly established, the attendance increased daily.

So many persons also applied for admission into the congregation, that, before long, its numbers had risen to one hundred and thirty.

The portion of the building appropriated to the fathers was now too small to accommodate them all and therefore, in the year 1581, they became desirous of making some addition to it. Just then, the Franciscan convent, which adjoined their church, fell vacant, and the fathers thought of buying it. But Philip objected to their incurring a fresh debt of more than five thousand crowns, which was the price of the convent, till they had paid off all the debt still owing for the building of the church. At the same time he expressed the greatest confidence that God would provide suitable accommodation for them. However, notwithstanding Philip's opinion, the fathers were so much afraid that some other purchaser for the adjoining convent might appear, that they opened a negotiation for the purchase, and the terms being agreed on, it only remained for the deed of sale to be signed. But as they were about to affix their signatures, a most unexpected difficulty arose; for the judge, without whose consent nothing could be done, refused to accept a bill in payment, and insisted on having the money paid down; and though the nuns were quite satisfied to have a bill, he stuck so firmly to his point, that the fathers being unable to raise the ready money, were forced to break off the bargain. When Philip heard of the transaction, he exclaimed: "God be praised! Those fathers will do things according to their own judgment; but mark my words, they will never buy the convent." And so indeed it came to pass, for on the 14th July of the same year Cardinal Cesi bought it, and on the 15th of January following, he gave it to the fathers.

For many years after the foundation of the Congregation, Philip continued to live at St. Girolamo, for his old habit of perseverance made him unwilling to quit the spot in which he had dwelt for thirty years, and in which he had borne so many crosses; besides which, he feared lest if he removed to the Vallicella, he should be regarded as the founder of the Congregation, and he could never believe that such an honour was his due, since, as he used to say, God and our Blessed Lady had founded it. In vain did his sons beseech him to come and live as a father among them; no entreaties could stir him out of his favourite nook, and he told them plainly that he would never move of his own will. At length they had recourse through Cardinal Cesi to the Pope, Gregory XIII, who, finding their desire a reasonable one, sent Philip an obedience to join the Congregation. This settled the matter, and on the 22nd November, the feast of St. Cecilia, A.D. 1583, Philip made his final move to the Vallicella, and took up his abode among his sons.

In course of time, the fame of the Oratory spread through Italy, and petitions came from various places requesting Philip to found similar congregations in them. The first of these was from Naples, and accordingly, A.D. 1586, Philip sent Tarugi and several other fathers to Naples, where, with the authority of the archbishop, they established a congregation on the same plan and with the same spiritual exercises as that at Rome, and before very long it numbered no less than seventy members.

The next congregation was founded in St. Severino in La Marca; and after that, so many others were established in various places, that Philip thought it desirable to make a new rule, to the effect that no Oratories, except those of Naples and St. Severino, should be connected with that of Rome; but as he did not wish to limit his congregations to these places, strangers were allowed to be admitted temporarily into the Roman Oratory, in order to learn its customs, with a view to founding congregations on their return to their several countries; and the Roman fathers might also be sent for a limited time to found Oratories in other places, on the condition that, as soon as they had finished their task they should return to their original home in Rome. The only exception which has been made to this rule, has been in the case of the Oratory of Lanciano in the Abruzzi, which was founded by Father Pompeo Pateri, A.D. 1598, on some property belonging to the Roman congregation. In the year 1766, there were above a hundred congregations of the Oratory of St. Philip in Europe and the East Indies; but since the revolutions of the last seventy years, many of these have ceased to exist, while, on the contrary, within the last twelve years two have been established in England.

Santa Maria in Vallicella, "Chiesa Nuova"

Chiesa Nuova, interior.

Chiesa Nuova, Ceiling and High Altar

The Deposition of Christ
Michaelangelo Merisi da Caravaggio

This painting, now in the Vatican Museums, was originally commissioned for the Chiesa Nuova. It hung at a side altar, and during Mass, when the priest elevated the host, it would line up directly with Christ's body in the painting. The painting was stolen by Napoleon, and when returned went to the Vatican Museums. A replica now hangs where the original once did.

CHAPTER XXV

AFTER the foundation of the Congregation of the Oratory, twenty years yet remained to St. Philip; and, if one may be permitted to speculate on the motives of God's providence, his life seems to have been prolonged during those twenty years specially in order to show forth the triumphs of Divine grace over the weakness of human nature. His life was indeed a wonderful one; for it might be said, in the words of the Canticle, that grace seemed to hang like the dew in his locks, and to drop like myrrh from his fingers, so that the daily course of his words and actions was a succession of supernatural and miraculous acts, which carried the beholders back to the Apostolic age. In the lives of most other saints, miracles stand out as isolated facts, but in Philip's life at this period, they were of such frequent occurrence and every action was so completely supernatural, that the Apostle's words: "I live, yet not I, but Christ liveth in me," might be literally applied to him.

A penitent was in pain; Philip placed his hands on his head, and the pain fled. Another was at the point of death; Philip prayed for him, and he recovered. Another was absent and in great distress of mind; Philip appeared to him and consoled him. Another had become delirious without having received the last sacraments, or arranged his worldly affairs; Philip came to see him, and the brain resumed its functions till the dying man had made his last preparations; when delirium returned, and he died. Another was troubled with temptations which he concealed, and Philip declared them to him. A young man wished to enter religion, and went to consult Philip; but before he spoke, Philip told him his thought, and revealed to him the will of God. The plague broke out at Milan; but before a single case occurred Philip foresaw it, and recalled his sons who were in that city. St. Catherine de' Ricci lived and died at Prato, while Philip never quitted Rome; but she told Giovanni Animuccia, the master of the Pope's chapel, that he had paid her a visit in the spirit; and, when Animuccia repeated her statement to Philip, he confirmed it, and on her death gave a most accurate description of her features. Philip told a penitent that if he went to Naples he would either be taken captive by the Turks, or be surely drowned. The young man went, and on the passage the vessel in which he sailed was attacked by the Turks, and, as the sole means of escape, he jumped into the sea, and was on the point of sinking, when, recalling Philip's words, he invoked his aid; and lo! instantly the saint appeared, and, taking him by the hair, placed him in safety on the shore.

Such things as these were of hourly occurrence; and besides these there were his daily ecstasies at Mass, and his constant state of rapturous union with God; so that it almost seemed as if, while his body continued to live and move upon earth, his spirit had been emancipated from all earthly ties, and had already taken its place in the celestial paradise.

Still, amid the great variety of supernatural gifts which God dispenses among His saints, there is one on which He seems to place a peculiar value, since it is bestowed on only a chosen few; and this is the power of raising the dead. But even this surpassing privilege was granted to St. Philip. The following are the circumstances in which he exercised it.

Among Philip's penitents, none stood higher in his friendship than the princely family of the Massimi. Their vineyard was his favourite resting place when he made the pilgrimage of the Seven Churches. Fabrizio de' Massimi and his first wife, Lavinia de' Rustici, were among his earliest penitents, as was also Porzia de' Massimi, wife of Giovanni Battista Salviati. Fabrizio's name has often occurred in these pages in connection with various circumstances, which show that he never took any important step without consulting Philip; and all his children grew up under Philip's eye. But his eldest son, Paolo, enjoyed a peculiar share of Philip's affection; for he had foretold his birth, and given him his name, and had heard his confessions from his earliest childhood; and up to the age of fourteen he had kept him pure and innocent as a child of St. Philip ought to be.

It came to pass that on the 10th January, A.D. 1583, Paolo fell ill of fever, and, in spite of all the care that was lavished on him, he continued to get worse and worse till the middle of March, when it was evident that he had not much longer to live. Philip went every day to see him, and the boy was so patient and happy through his long illness, that Philip must have rejoiced to think he was being taken to paradise while his baptismal robe was pure from spot or stain of sin; but still he had a longing to be with him at the last, and he gave strict injunctions to the family to send for him when Paolo should be dying.

Accordingly, on the morning of March 16th, Francesca, the faithful servant who had watched over Paolo from his birth, went to St. Girolamo to summon Philip; but when she got there he was saying Mass, and she could not speak to him. As soon as his Mass was over, they told him Francesca's errand, and he set out instantly for the palace of the Massimi. But he arrived too late; for, half an hour before he came, Paolo had breathed his last in the presence of the priest who had given him extreme unction, and who had since left the house; and now Francesca was about to wash the corpse, and dress it in its grave-clothes.

At the top of the stairs Philip met Fabrizio, who said to

him with tears: "Paolo is dead." Philip answered not a word, but, passing him by, went into the room where the boy was stretched out dead, and, throwing himself on the bed, lay there for seven or eight minutes, trembling from the palpitation of his heart, as was his wont when he was in fervent prayer. Then rising, he took some holy water and sprinkled the corpse, throwing some of the water into the mouth, after which he breathed on the face, and pressing his hands on the forehead, cried with a loud voice: "Paolo! Paolo!" At these words the boy opened his eyes as if waking from sleep, and answered: "Father," adding, after a pause: "I had forgotten one sin, and I wish to confess it." So Philip put a crucifix into Paolo's hand, and every one having left the room, he heard his confession, and gave him absolution. When the family returned Philip was talking to Paolo about his mother and one of his sisters, both of whom were dead; and, during the conversation, which lasted half an hour, Paolo answered distinctly, and looked as fresh and rosy as if he had never been ill. At last Philip asked him if he was willing to die, and he answered: "Yes." Then Philip asked him a second time if he was willing to die, and he again answered: "Yes, very willing; for I want to see my mother and my sister in paradise." So Philip gave him his blessing, saying: "Go, then, God bless you, and pray for me;" and instantly, without the least movement, but with a calm and joyful look, Paolo once more expired in Philip's arms. These facts were attested on oath by Fabrizio de' Massimi, Violante Santa Croce, his second wife, and Francesca, the servant, who were eye-witnesses of them.

But if, in spite of all these miracles, there had yet been found any so unbelieving as to doubt the power of Divine grace, Philip's humility alone would have sufficed to prove it. In the same proportion as God became united to him, his knowledge of his own nothingness became deeper and clearer; for the effulgence of the Divine glory within him so illumined his soul, that the infirmities of his human nature looked like dark spots on the face of the noonday sun; and hence he so completely realized the deep truth contained in the words: "Not I, but Christ liveth in me," that he appeared to himself but as the earthly channel through which flows a golden stream, or as the worthless vessel into which a costly liquor is poured. His greatest distress was, that others could not be convinced of this, but would persist in fancying that he was something more than an ordinary man. They would ask him for something of his, "because they knew he was a saint," and in vain would he angrily exclaim: "Begone; I am a devil and not a saint." Or, when he was ill, they would suggest to him the prayer of St. Martin: "If I am necessary to Thy people, I refuse not labour;" and it would be useless for him to reprove them by saying: "I am not St. Martin, and I never thought I was; and, if I believed that I was necessary to any one, I should consider myself damned." In spite of all his efforts, they would still hold to their own opinion; and sometimes, when they looked on the great gifts with which God had endowed him, they would remark: "Father, saints do great things;" and then, as if in despair of convincing them of the truth, he would meekly correct them by replying: "Do not say that, but rather say, that God does great things in His saints."

This contest, which he was always carrying on with those around him, produced a change in his outward conduct, which would have been strange in common men, but which is easily accounted for by the extraordinary humility and peculiar position of a saint. In his younger days he had moved among the crowd as one of themselves, avoiding unnecessary singularity, and all that could attract notice to himself; and this was the spirit of the lessons of humility which he gave his spiritual children. But now he used purposely to do many extravagant and ridiculous things, partly in hopes of convincing them that he was more foolish, vile, and contemptible than others, and thus teaching them to distinguish between himself, poor sinner that he was, and the wonderful works which God was pleased to work through him; and partly in order to mortify any secret pleasure, which might perchance have been excited by the extraordinary veneration which met him on all sides.

He seldom went into public without doing something which might cause him to be despised and laughed at. At one time he had half of his beard shaved off, and went about with only half a beard. At another, he made one of the brothers cut his hair and beard where a number of people were passing by, and, when they stopped to look, he would say: "Look now, does not he cut my hair very well?" Cardinal Gesualdo having given him a fur pelisse, and made him promise to wear it, he wore it for a month over his habit, and, as he walked through the streets, he strutted along like a peacock, looking down at himself with admiration. He would often stop the water-carriers, and, asking them to let him have a drink, would put his mouth to the barrels and drink, much to the surprise of the passers-by, who would wonder to see a respectable person drink in that way. As he walked through the principal thoroughfares, he would dance and jump, or run and leap, and when he had taken a good leap down two or three steps, he would look round, as if he were quite delighted with himself, exclaiming: "What do you think of that?" And then he would be not a little pleased if, as sometimes happened, the bystanders cried out: "Look at that madman." Sometimes he would carry in his hand a large bunch of flowers, which he would be constantly smelling with a conceited air; and at other times he would read aloud as he went along, making all sorts of mistakes to lead people to remark how ignorant he was. He would often go about Rome wearing a pair of white shoes; or he would wear a red shirt when distinguished persons called on him; or he would go into the church with a coat turned wrong side out over his habit, and his baretta cocked on one side.

He did such things as these more especially on those occasions when greater gravity and decorum might have been expected from him; and at such times he had the additional motive that these mortifications served as distractions to keep down the overflowings of the supernatural emotions which might otherwise have overpowered him. For instance, on the Feast of our Lady's Nativity, which is the principal feast of the Chiesa Nuova, the choir at vespers being filled with cardinals and prelates, he appeared in a most extravagant costume, hoping that some of them would reprove him; but they, seeing through his saintly motive, all rose to receive him, and made room for him to sit down among them; whereupon he smiled and answered: "I may as well sit down among your attendants;" and, sitting down among the latter, he remained there during the rest of vespers. Also on the occasion of the translation of the bodies of SS. Papias and Maurus, while he was standing at the door of the church awaiting the arrival of the procession, there happened to stand near him one of the Pope's Swiss guards, who had a very handsome beard; whereupon he went up to the man, and began to stroke his beard, with gestures of silly admiration, to the diversion of some of the crowd; though others, who understood him better, were greatly edified.

Another favourite occasion for such acts of mortification was, when strangers were attracted by the fame of his sanctity to visit him; and for such times he kept by him several books of jests and foolish stories, which he would then read with great apparent interest. Once some Polish noblemen called on him, hoping to have some profitable conversation; but while they were coming up the stairs, he ordered Father Consolini to read one of these books, and not to stop till he told him. As soon as the noblemen entered the room, he said quite unceremoniously to them: "Pray wait till this story is finished;" and while Consolini continued to read, he exclaimed from time to time: "Have not I got nice books, and have not I profitable things read to me?" Meanwhile the noblemen looked at each other in amazement; and at last they went away, not a little disappointed at the conduct of one whom they had been led to suppose was a great saint. As soon as they were gone, Philip bade Father Consolini close the book, saying: "We have done all that was necessary."

On another occasion, as he was calling on the Marchioness Rangona, he met the Spanish ambassadress, who, after some conversation, asked him how long it was since he had left the world. To which he answered: "I am not aware that I have ever left it;" and he then proceeded to tell her about the story-books and jest-books which he had in his room; after which, turning to Father Antonio Gallonio, who accompanied him, he said: "You can say, Antonio, how fond I am of nice books of poetry and stories." But Gallonio replied: "What wonder, Father, since you cannot in any other way temper the flames of the love of God." When they returned home, Philip reproved Gallonio for this answer, saying: "That was a pretty answer, indeed, that you gave me! God forgive you! What could you be thinking of, that you said such a thing?"

But notwithstanding all his eccentricities, Philip could not conceal the fact that he was a great saint. As he walked through the streets, or passed through the church, people would kneel down to receive his blessing and kiss the hem of his habit. The first nobles in Rome thought it an honour to make his bed, or sweep his room, or clean his shoes. His penitents revered his words as heaven-inspired oracles; the members of his congregation treasured up his hair and all that belonged to him, as precious relics, and some even went so far as to invoke him as a saint while he was still alive. His sanctity was held to be undoubted by all the religious bodies in Rome, the most distinguished members of which would prostrate themselves before him, and speak publicly of him as a saint and "a living relic," regulating their conduct on all important occasions according to his advice. The cardinals, with one voice, bore witness to his sanctity; successive Popes spoke openly of him as a saint, and treated him with reverence, not allowing him to kiss their foot, or to remain standing and uncovered in their presence; and even the great saints who were his contemporaries—St. Ignatius, St. Charles Borromeo, St. Camillus of Lellis, St. Felix Cantalice, and many others,—united in proclaiming him to be a saint.

As to worldly honours and wealth, canonries, bishoprics, pensions, and even the cardinal's hat, were offered him again and again; but he cared not for these earthly prizes, and always declined them. Moreover, since he knew that there is as much, or even more honour in refusing dignities than in accepting them, he was careful to refuse them in such a way that it might not even be known that they had been offered to him. Gregory XIV, in the presence of several persons, placed on his head the cardinal's cap, which he had himself worn as cardinal, saying to him: "We make you a cardinal." But Philip going up to the Pope, whispered a few words in his ear, after which he treated the whole matter as a joke; and, on going away, he left the cardinal's cap behind him. And when the Pope sent the cap after him with the same words as before, he continued to take it all as a joke, sending back his thanks to his Holiness, and that he would let him know when he should be glad to accept the dignity. Clement VIII also pressed him over and over again to be a cardinal, saying to him, when he came to see him on his accession: "Now you will not be able to help being a cardinal," and continuing to solicit him to accept the dignity even up to the time of his death.

But Philip had placed his ambition far above such poor honours as these, and he would have nothing to do with them. On one occasion, when some of his penitents had been talking to him on this subject, in connection with his intimacy with the Pope, he replied: "My sons, believe my words: I would pray God to send me death or to pierce me with an arrow, rather than that I should indulge even in the thought of these dignities. I do indeed desire the virtues and the devotion of the cardinals and the Pope, but not their greatness." On another occasion, he expressed the same feeling still more forcibly and touchingly to Bernardino Corona, one of the brothers of the Congregation. One day, about three months before his death, he said to him: "Bernardino, the Pope wishes to make me a cardinal. What do you say to it?" Whereupon Bernardino answered: "I think, father, you ought to accept the dignity, if for no other reason, yet at least for the good of the Congregation." But Philip, taking off his baretta and looking joyfully up to heaven, exclaimed: "Paradise! Paradise!"

CHAPTER XXVI

HILIP'S long life was now drawing to a close, and with it, the sixteenth century. What influence had he upon it? What was the result of his eighty years? Can we guess at the object which God had in view in raising up this most supernatural saint?

Certainly his power appears but very little on the surface of that most turbulent time. In reading his life, who could ever have supposed that he was the contemporary of so many men and women whose names are still as familiar to us as if they lived but yesterday? How strange a contrast are the great events of his time with the peaceful course of his existence upon earth! A rapid parallel between his life and contemporary history will bring out the difference.

St. Philip was born in the year 1515. It was in the pontificate of Leo X, in the midst of the struggle for dominion over the north of Italy between Francis I and Charles V. This places at once before our eyes the palmy days of Henry VIII and of Cardinal Wolsey. It was the bright period of the Renaissance; it was the year of the brilliant victory of the young French king at Marignano. This will serve to locate St. Philip's life in the century of which he saw within five years of the close. For the sake of convenience, his life may be divided into three periods: the first from his birth to his ordination; the second from the time when he became a priest, in 1551, at the age of 36, till the accession of Gregory XIII, in 1572; the third from that time till his death.

The first period was, on the whole, one, first, of terrible defeat, then of partial recovery for the Church; it was the time of the sack of Rome, of the Diet of Worms, of the loss of England to the Holy See. In the year that Philip left his beautiful Florence, and was spending his time in the lonely chapel before the miraculous crucifix of San Germano, Henry VIII married Anne Boleyn. He was studying at Rome in the Augustinian schools when news arrived there of the martyrdom of Cardinal Fisher, Sir Thomas More, and the Carthusians of the Charterhouse. Then came the mystic period of the Catacombs, and the no less mystic power exercised by the young layman over souls. In 1544 occurred his baptism of fire, in the deep subterranean galleries of St. Sebastian's, a solitude far more silent than the deserts of the Thebaid; in 1548 he began the "Trinità dei Pellegrini." During that decade of years which closed the first half-century, the world was far otherwise occupied. The war between Charles V and Francis I was finally burning itself out in the north of Italy. Death was removing from the world several of the chief actors in its troubled scene. Luther died in 1546; the sun of the young monarchs of the Field of the Cloth of Gold, which rose so promisingly, sunk in deep night in the year 1547. Thus the affairs of the Catholic Church seemed on the whole more flourishing: two of its worst enemies were carried away by death; St. Ignatius was appointed general of the Jesuits in 1541; the Council of Trent opened four years after; and Charles V apparently crushed the German Protestants at Muhlberg. Such was the state of the world when Philip was ordained priest.

Next comes the period of the formation of the Congregation. Rome became Philip's Indies in 1557. Then began the meetings in the little oratory, over the nave of St. Girolamo; and then the troubles from the Vicar-General of Paul IV. St. Giovanni dei Fiorentini was given to the infant community in 1564. Under Pius V, Philip continued to achieve the conquest of Rome, with partial intervals of tribulation, till 1572. Philip had his little troubles; but, while in spite of them he was winning his marvellous victories, what a war was raging in the world and in the Church! Were ever twenty years more momentous since the world began? England won back under Mary, lost under Elizabeth; Lutheranism resuscitated, and wresting half Germany by the treaty of Passau from the Catholic Church, while she is fighting for her very existence in France. The only bright spot of the time is the battle of Lepanto in 1571, and the whole reign of St. Pius V. Otherwise all is dark; it is the rampant period of French Protestantism gathering strength under the false, half-hearted kings of the race of Valois, whose policy oscillated between the indifferentism of edicts of toleration and the frantic improvisation of a massacre of St. Bartholomew. During all this time we know that Philip was at Rome, slowly building up the Oratory. We know that he must have said his Rosary on that day of October when the confraternities went in procession through the streets, while the Cross was encountering the Crescent on the waters of the Gulf of Corinth. We know that he must have rejoiced when the news came of the victories of Jarnac and of Moncontour, and have mourned over the death by an assassin's hand of the leader of the genuine Catholic party, Francis of Guise. All this, we are sure, he must necessarily have done, but not a trace of all these events is to be found in his life.

The last period consists of twenty-three years more spirit-stirring than ever. In 1585 the League breaks out, and with all its faults presents to the world the spectacle of a great nation entering into a voluntary association to defend the interests of the Catholic Church betrayed by its king. Two years after, Mary Stuart laid her head on the block at Fotheringay, while Henry IV began his marvellous career of victory at Coutras. Next year the Spanish Armada was destroyed. In 1590 Ivry was fought, and four years more of victory placed Henry of Navarre, a Catholic sovereign, on the throne of France. The chains of Protestantism were riveted on England, while France remained unconquerably Catholic. All this while Philip was quietly finishing his work. In 1576 Gregory XIII establishes the Oratory by a formal brief. Then the Vallicella is given to the Congregation. Then Philip builds the house and church of the Chiesa Nuova. In 1577 the Oratory leaves St. Giovanni dei Fiorentini, to which it had been transferred three years before from San Girolamo della Carità. Here thirteen peaceful years Philip lived, and then he died. He blessed the young Englishmen of the English College, which was so near the cradle of the Oratory; he addressed them in the words of the hymn on the Holy Innocents: "*Salvete flores martyrum,*" to bid them God-speed to what was then the land of martyrdom; but otherwise we read no trace of his influence on the final struggle of Catholicism in England. In one way, which we shall notice presently, his name is connected with affairs in France, but it was only when the battle had been fought, and was over. He enters into no great educational schemes, no vast movement of controversy, like the disciples of the great St. Ignatius. His direct influence on the public events of that wonderful sixteenth century was as little as could be. What then was St. Philip's work?

It is wonderful how little the policy and the arms of the Catholic party in Europe were successful. The invincible Armada was dashed to pieces on the coasts of Ireland. If the League preserved France for the Catholic cause, it was not because victory crowned its efforts. God did not choose that the Church should owe its safety to the success of the policy and the arms of the house of Austria. So it has been ever since. The Catholic Stuarts were beaten by Protestant Hanoverians; while the Catholic powers have never consulted the interests of the Church in their policy. The houses of France and Austria have ever been at war, while a French cardinal has let loose Protestant Sweden on Catholic Germany, and Austria has triumphed with the help of English arms. This is the characteristic of modern history—the absolute subordination of religion to national interests. In such a state of things, it would be in vain for the Church to hope for success by acting on the mediæval principle that Europe is Christian.

What then has God done? He has spread abroad, throughout the body of the Church, a spirit of love and devotedness far more general than had existed for ages before. The fire of the Holy Ghost has burst the bounds of the cloister, and has kindled the world. While the cloister itself has become more fervent, the number of those who, living in the secular state, are really seeking to love God perfectly, has increased to an extent of which St. Bernard never dreamed. The old mediæval type of the ordinary Christian who saved his soul by keeping the ten commandments, and communicating once a year, is no longer the ideal of Christian secular life. God has rewarded that part of Europe which remained faithful amidst the falling away of the sixteenth century by a wonderful effusion of the Holy Spirit, of which the gentle treatment of sinners in the confessional and the frequent reception of the Holy Communion are the measure and the proof.

It was to be the Apostle of the perfect love of God and of prayer, among those who live in the world, that God raised up Philip. For this, the Holy Spirit kindled his heart with fire; for this He made him the most supernatural of saints, so that his whole life seemed to be rather in heaven than on earth. For this He furnished him with a strange power over all hearts, and a most astonishing insight into the most secret thoughts of souls. It was in Rome that he exercised this blessed apostolate; and in order to appreciate the work which God enabled him to accomplish, it will be necessary for us to compare the state of Rome when he arrived there, with what it was when he had completed his task.

The history of the Roman people during the middle ages, plainly declares their ferocity, their turbulence, and their proud intolerance of control. It was little more than a succession of popular tumults, of conspiracies, of schisms, and rebellions, which sometimes made the Pope a fugitive from fortress to fortress in his own dominions, and at others drove him to seek an asylum with foreign princes; while even in the best of times, he exercised within the city a sovereignty, which depended rather on the sufferance of his subjects than on his own independent power. To such a height had matters come in the beginning of the fourteenth century, that, A.D. 1305, Clement V took up his abode in Avignon, which for above seventy years was the seat of the papacy, while Rome was left a prey to its internal dissensions, and to the cruel tyranny of its fierce nobles. At length the entreaties of the repentant Romans, and still more the influence of St. Catherine of Siena, induced Gregory XI to return to Rome, A.D. 1376. But the promise of peace was of short duration; for on the death of Gregory two years after, the Great Schism, as it is called, broke out, and for forty years popes and antipopes were elected in quick succession; and such a strange state of confusion prevailed, that it was no easy matter for Catholics to know to whom to offer their spiritual allegiance. At length the Council of Constance cut the Gordian knot, by receiving the resignation of all the rival popes and electing in their stead Otho Colonna, who took the name of Martin V and established the papal chair once more at Rome, A.D. 1420. Truly did the Cardinal Giles of Viterbo say: "that up to this time the Romans had never been subdued or reduced to submission, whether by arms, or by emperors, or by barbarian conquerors, and so many wars, and armies, and conflagrations, and sackings, and anathemas, year after year, and century after century, had all worked in vain to bring them into a state of true subordination."[22]

The state of the city when Martin V returned to it, may be considered as representing the condition of its inhabitants. Rome of the fifteenth century bore no resemblance to that gorgeous and magnificent Rome which the imagination loves to evoke from its splendid ruins, nor to the beauty and sacred majesty of the city which now crowns the seven hills. The ancient basilicas, the churches, the convents, the palaces of the Cæsars, the splendid trophies of Imperial times, the sacred monuments of early Christian ages, and the frowning fortresses of feudal nobles, were all alike crumbling to ruins. Rome was become a mere dwelling of herdsmen, in no way superior to the peasants of the surrounding Campagna. The hills were uninhabited, and the population was limited to the low levels along the windings of the Tiber; the streets were narrow and unpaved; the tottering houses were supported by buttresses; cattle wandered at large; wild ducks made their nests in the marshy ground; the Capitol had become the "hill of goats," and the Forum was the "cow's field."[23]

On the return of the Papal court, a new population flocked to Rome; but many a long year elapsed before the city rose from its ruins, and still longer before its inhabitants became worthy to dwell in the capital of Christendom. Successive popes, from Nicholas V to Julius II and Leo X, laboured successfully to restore the city to her ancient beauty and majesty; but the fierce spirit of the Roman still

---

[22] Rohrbaeker, *Hist. de l'Eglise Cath.* l. 81.

[23] Ranke's *Hist. of the Popes*, 1. 4, sect. 8.

remained unsubdued. Civil wars, factions, violence, and endless discord, raged as before. The population was divided into Guelfs and Ghibellines, a Spanish faction and a French one, the partisans of the several noble families, of the provincial municipalities, of the different Italian states, of the reigning Pope, and of his predecessors, with numberless other parties springing out of family feuds or private interests, each and all of whom were ready to rush to arms on the slightest provocation. It was no vulgar rabble who had to be civilized and held in check by superior intelligence or force; but it was princes, and nobles, and prelates, who had to be brought into subjection to the law of humanity and of the gospel. In the year 1492, on the death of Innocent VIII, the bishop Leonelli, who delivered the funeral oration, urged the speedy choice of a successor: "because," said he: "there is not an hour of the day in which Rome is not the theatre of murder and rapine;"[24] and in the next few weeks two hundred murders were committed by the first families in the city.

It was to the conversion of this fierce and wicked population that Philip was called, and such was their state when he came to Rome. A few years before, things had arrived at their lowest ebb, Adrian VI had attempted, A.D. 1522-3, to stem the torrent, but had failed; for the very persons to whom it belonged to enforce the observance of the laws and to inculcate religion and morality, took the lead in defying and outraging them. Then came the sack of Rome by the Imperial troops under Bourbon, A.D. 1527; and men's hearts were touched by the judgments of God, and they woke from their dream to a vague consciousness that all was amiss, and that something must be done to remedy the crying evils. But still they were far from perceiving that the only true reform must be a personal one; they had much to

---

[24] Rohrbacker, *Hist. de l'Eglise Cath.* l. 83.

learn before the proud Roman spirit would submit to be controlled; and the great danger was, that when the first movements of compunction had exhausted themselves, they might relapse into their former sins, and become only the more hardened by the neglect of God's warning voice.

The year after Philip came to Rome, A.D. 1534, Paul III ascended the Papal throne. The critical position of the Catholic Church, consequent on the outbreak of Protestantism in Germany, diverted Paul's attention in great measure from the less urgent necessities of the Roman court; but still the Church owes him a debt of gratitude for two acts, which laid a solid foundation for future reform. The first was the choice of his cardinals; for instead of being influenced by political or personal motives, he selected, for their merits alone, Contarini, Caraffa, Pole, and several others, all of them deeply imbued with the spirit of reform, and most of them members of the Oratory of Divine Love, an association which had been formed some years before for the promotion of greater strictness of life. The other was the definition of the faith on the points connected with the Protestant heresy, at the earlier sittings of the council of Trent, with a clearness and decision which have rendered further doubt impossible.

During Paul's reign, Philip was living in Rome as an obscure layman, leading his solitary life in the churches and catacombs, or pursuing his eager search for souls in the shops and squares, and public thoroughfares. His only motives were the glory of God and the salvation of sinners; yet each soul that he won to God, was a step towards the reformation of the city; and though his work advanced slowly, and his sphere was a humble one, yet his persevering labours from year to year were sure in time to bring forth their fruit. The year before Paul's death, A.D. 1548, the Confraternity of the Santissima Trinità was founded, and the Quarant' Ore was introduced into Rome. This devotion, which is at all times singularly attractive, must have been doubly so in Rome at a period when public worship had been stripped of its due solemnity, and when preaching was very rare. The simple addresses of Philip to the assembled worshippers could not fail to touch the hearts of many, while the long silent hours spent in adoration before the Blessed Sacrament, were well calculated to impress the thoughtless, and to lead the soul into that interior solitude in which she stands face to face with God, and hears that small still voice which convinces her "of sin, and of justice, and of judgment." Two years after, the Confraternity opened its house for the reception of pilgrims, and the success which attended this work of charity, proves that already the spirit of worldliness and selfishness, which had long reigned in Rome, was beginning to give way.

Julius III succeeded to the Papal chair A.D. 1549. During his pontificate Philip took holy orders and went to live at St. Girolamo. From this time his sphere was enlarged; and though he dreamt not of taking a part in the great work of reformation, yet as men of rank and station were one after another drawn within his influence, an impartial observer could not have failed to perceive that the movement was passing upwards, and must soon reach the highest ranks of the nobility and clergy. Many years, however, had yet to elapse before the fruit of his labours should appear.

Both Marcellus II and Paul IV strove zealously to introduce a new order of things in Rome; but so little impression did they make on their turbulent subjects, that as soon as Paul's death became known, a mob assembled to insult his memory. They tore his statue from its pedestal, broke it to pieces, and dragged the head with the triple crown through the streets; they set fire to the Inquisition, maltreated its officers, and threatened to burn down the

Dominican convent of the Minerva; and, as in old times, the rioters were led, not by a vulgar demagogue, but by the Colonnas, the Orsini, the Cesarini, the Massimi, and others of the first nobles in Rome.

It was in Paul's pontificate, that Philip received his mission and began his work systematically. We have seen that the meetings in the Oratory, and the pilgrimages to the Seven Churches, did not escape the vigilance of the pontiff, and that after due examination, they received his sanction. Under Paul's successor, Pius IV, Philip came more prominently forward, for he was the personal friend of both the Pope and his nephew, St. Charles Borromeo, and no great step was taken by either without his advice being sought. Still so gentle and unostentatious was his course, that it might well have been questioned whether his life would leave a trace behind for future generations, or whether his labours would ever be known till the Great Day when the secrets of all hearts shall be revealed.

Thus three-and-thirty years glided by, and Philip worked on humbly and perseveringly. But at length the fruit approached maturity; a new era dawned on Rome, and a saint sat once more in the apostle's chair. From his childhood Michele Ghislieri, generally known as St. Pius V, gave signs of his future sanctity. He entered the Dominican order when only fourteen, and from that time he sought the lowest place, while he aspired to the practice of the highest virtue. He held various offices in his order, in all of which he was remarkable for his love of poverty and monastic discipline. He was appointed to an office in the Inquisition A.D. 1534, and was distinguished for his zeal for the faith, and the unflinching courage with which he faced the dangers to which the discharge of his duty often exposed him. The Conte della Trinità having threatened to throw him into a well, he calmly replied: "As to that, it shall be as

God pleases." When he became a cardinal he made no change in his mode of life. He formed his establishment on the lowest scale consistent with propriety; he told his servants that in entering his service they must consider themselves to be entering a monastery, and he proceeded to regulate his household accordingly.

He carried the same spirit to the papal throne. He wore his coarse monk's habit under the purple; he slept on the hard straw bed which his rule enjoined; he observed all the fasts of the Church most rigorously, and was so frugal at other times that the expenses of his table did not exceed about eightpence a day. He attended Mass daily, and generally said it himself; on solemn occasions he might be seen walking in religious processions, barefoot and bareheaded, with a look of unaffected piety which touched all beholders; every night he interrupted his brief repose by going down to the church of St. Peter, and making the round of the altars; and when any important matter was pending, he would spend the whole night in prayer. Instead of armorial bearings, his seal bore the text: "*Utinam dirigantur viæ ad custodiendas justificationes tuas;*"[25] and, in order that the calls of his high position might not detach his thoughts from the sufferings of our Lord, he always kept on the table before him a crucifix, round which were the words: "*Absit mihi gloriari, nisi in cruce Domini Jesu Christi!*"[26]

It was customary, on the accession of a pope, to scatter among the populace large sums of money, which fell into the hands of the strong and active, while the sick and needy were left unrelieved. St. Pius forbade this practice, and ordered that the usual sum should be carefully distributed in the poorest quarters of the town among the most

---

[25] "Would that my paths be directed to guard thy justices." -Editor.

[26] "Far be it for me to boast, except in the cross of the Lord Jesus Christ." -Editor.

necessitous and deserving. He also refused to give the usual
entertainment to the foreign ambassadors who were present
at his coronation, but sent the thousand crowns, which were
generally expended in this way, to the poorest convents;
and, when he was told that some persons had taken his
conduct amiss, he replied: "God will not punish me for
having deprived the envoys of princes of a feast, but He will
call me to account for the necessities of His own poor
members."

He long refused to make his nephew a cardinal, and at
last he was induced to do so only because it was represented
to him that it would facilitate his discourse with foreign
courts. But he could never be persuaded to raise any other
members of his family beyond the middle ranks. Moreover,
he issued a bull forbidding any future alienation of church
property; and in order to secure its observance by his
successors, he required all the cardinals to take an oath to
maintain it, and declared every one excommunicate who
should seek or counsel a dispensation from it.

The example which he set in his own person he enjoined
on his household, his court, and his capital. His household
was ordered according to the strictest discipline. Three times
a week a sermon was preached to them, and every night
they were assembled for prayers, after which the pope
retired to his apartment, and the gates of the palace were as
strictly closed as if it had been a convent. Having assembled
the cardinals and principal members of the curia, he
exhorted them in the most solemn terms to amend each his
own life and conscience, reminding them that they were
called by our Lord to be the light of the world. New editions
of the Breviary and Missal were issued; all bishops were
required to subscribe the Creed of Pope Pius IV; and the
Catechism of the Council of Trent was completed and
published A.D. 1566. St. Pius also published several bulls

enforcing discipline in the religious orders and among the secular clergy, against blasphemy, for the observance of Sunday, and one forbidding physicians to visit any patient confined to his bed for more than three days, without being certified that the sick man had confessed his sins anew. He also made some very severe laws against Jewish astrologers and women of light character; and, when some persons remonstrated with him, and besought him to be more lenient to the latter, he indignantly replied: "I would rather remove my chair from Rome than remain in the city with them."

To St. Pius' energy, but still more to his prayers, Christendom owes the victory of Lepanto, which broke the naval power of the Turks. The formation of a league to drive them out of Europe was a great object of his desires, and his death alone prevented its completion. The restoration of England to the Church was also frequently in his thoughts. He promised at one time to spend large treasures, and even to melt down the crucifixes and chalices, if necessary, in order to fit out an expedition, at the head of which he would march in person. When he felt the approach of death, he set out on a pilgrimage to the Seven Churches, and on his way happening to meet some English refugees, he stopped and said to them, that he would "fain pour out his blood for their sakes." He expired May 2nd, 1572.

The impulse which St. Pius had given to religion was not allowed to die out with him. He was succeeded by Gregory XIII, who not only set before him the example of his saintly predecessor, but determined, if possible, to surpass him. Gregory was the intimate friend of St. Philip; he said Mass at least three times a week, never omitting it on Sunday; he evinced the greatest anxiety that all his appointments to bishoprics should tend to the glory of God; and in all other respects he was a pattern of exemplary piety. His chief attention was given to the encouragement of education. He founded the English College at Rome, and also a Greek College for the education of Greeks in communion with the Roman see. His liberality to the Jesuits seemed to have no bounds. He gave them a foundation for their Roman College, which has justly been styled the Seminary of all nations. He may also be regarded as the founder of the German College, since it was falling to decay for want of means, when he largely endowed it. Twenty-two Jesuit colleges owed their origin to him, and it has been said that there was not a Jesuit school in the world to which he did not contribute in some way or other.

Sixtus V succeeded Gregory A.D. 1585. He was a Franciscan, and, as Fra Felice Peretti, had been the reformer of his order. St. Pius V was his patron; St. Philip was his intimate friend; and a high Catholic tone characterized all his actions.

Gregory XIV was a friend of Philip, who had foretold his election; but when the cardinals came to announce to him his election, they found him in his cell in prayer before a crucifix. He was a man of pure and blameless spirit; he said Mass daily, repeated his office on his knees, fasted twice a week, and found his recreation in the works of St. Bernard, or in St. Philip's little room. He was so simple-minded that people used to say in jest that he had not enough of the world in his composition.

Clement VIII also was the friend and disciple of St. Philip. He confessed every evening and said Mass every day at noon. He fasted twice a week, wore a hair shirt, slept on straw, and often visited the churches barefoot. Daily twelve poor men dined in the room with himself, and before sitting down to table, he always waited on them and served them; while at the jubilee, A.D. 1600, he set the example of visiting the pilgrims at the Santissima Trinità, and performing the most menial offices for them. His application to business was indefatigable, and during his brief intervals of recreation, he would read St. Bernard's works, or send for some of the Oratory Fathers to come and discuss some point of theology. He was so much attached to Philip, that he wished to have him for his confessor; but no entreaty could induce the aged saint to accept the dignity, and Baronius was appointed in his stead.

The same religious spirit which had thus taken possession of the papal throne, pervaded the whole society of Rome. It would carry us far beyond our limits to notice the host of saints, St. Ignatius, St. Aloysius, St. Stanislaus Kotska, St. Camillus, St. Felix Cantalice, and many others, who were during St. Philip's life to be met in the streets of Rome. Among the cardinals, first and foremost, stood St. Charles Borromeo. His nephew, Cardinal Frederick Borromeo, was scarcely his inferior in virtue. Cardinal Ottavio Paravicini was educated under St. Philip's eye, living with the Fathers at St. Giovanni; and even after he was a cardinal, his greatest pleasure was to perform the most menial services for the aged saint. Cardinal Agostino Valerio, whose learning was extraordinary, was the model of a primitive bishop. Cardinal Salviati was noted for his simple, blameless life, and his austere virtues; while Cardinal Mandruzzi was called the Cato of the college. Cardinal Sirleto was so eminent in science that he superintended the reformation of the calendar, and his general attainments obtained for him the title of a living library; but so simple were his habits and so great his love of souls, that he would often leave his books, collect round him the boys who sold wood in the market, give them religious instruction, and then buy their wood. Cardinal San Severina so far surpassed in strictness even all these, that, on the ground of his austerity alone, he lost his election to the papal throne;

while, on the other hand, Cardinal Tosco was said to have lost his only because he occasionally used certain expressions, which, though common in Lombardy, were offensive to the severer tone of the Roman court.

All who rose to eminence, whether in law, learning, poetry, or the arts, were characterized by the same religious spirit. Baronius, the great historian of the day, was, as we have seen, a Father of the Oratory; Bellarmine, the celebrated theologian, and Maffei, the historian, were Jesuits; Mantica and Arigone, auditors of the Rota and celebrated jurists, were also remarkable for the sanctity of their lives. Muret, the first Latin scholar of the day, spent great part of his life in expounding the Pandects; but in his old age he took holy orders, said Mass daily, and devoted himself to the study of theology. Azpilcueta, the great Spanish casuist, whose decisions were regarded as oracles throughout Europe, spent his leisure hours in waiting on the sick in the hospitals. The spirit of the times may also be traced in the religious tone of Tasso's poetry, in the paintings of Guido, Domenichino, and the Caracci, where the close imitation of nature is happily united with the expression of religious sentiment; and above all, in the music of Palestrina, to whom belongs the glory of having anew consecrated this art to the service of God and the Church.[27]

At this time, too, numerous religious orders sprang up,

---

[27] Church music had become so utterly unsuited to its purpose, that it was gravely discussed whether it should not be banished from Divine worship. It was declared necessary that the music should be in harmony with the words, but the professors of the art declared this to be impracticable. St. Charles Borromeo called on Palestrina to exert his skill and decide the question. Palestrina made two attempts and failed. His third was the Mass of Pope Marcellus, and when it was performed before Pius IV, his Holiness was enchanted, and compared it to the heavenly strains which St. John heard in his Apocalyptic vision.

while the old ones were reformed. First, in undisputed preeminence, stood the Society of Jesus, founded in the pontificate of Paul III. St. Charles Borromeo founded the Congregation of Oblates of St. Ambrose; St. Camillus of Lellis, that of Ministers of the Sick; St. Francis Caracciolo, the Clerks Minors; the Venerable Giovanni Leonardi, the Clerks Regular of the Mother of God; and Enrico Pietra, the Association of Christian Doctrine. At the same time, the Franciscans were reformed by Fra Felice Peretti, afterwards Sixtus V, and the Dominicans and all the other orders in Rome, acquired fresh vigour.

The same religious fervour was visible amid the masses of the people. Paolo Tiepolo, writing from Rome, A.D. 1576, says,—"Several pontiffs in succession have been men of blameless lives, and this has contributed immeasurably to the welfare of the Church; for all other men have become better, or at least have assumed the appearance of being so. Cardinals and prelates attend diligently at Mass; their households are careful to avoid whatever might give offence. The whole city has indeed put off its former recklessness of manner. People are all more Christian-like in life and habit than they formerly were. It may even be safely affirmed that, in matters of religion, Rome is not far from as high a degree of perfection as human nature is permitted to attain to."

There is also extant a letter written from Rome, April 9th, A.D. 1566, by a German nobleman to a German prince,[28] which describes in greater detail the wonderful change that had come over society at Rome. The writer had arrived in Rome, filled with the prejudices that had been excited in Germany by his countrymen, who had visited the Holy City in the beginning of the century, when, indeed, there was ample ground for scandal; and he expected, as he himself

[28] Rohrbacker, *Hist. de l'Eglise Cath.* l. 86, Apud Bzovium 1566, p. 34.

says, to find piety, religion, and morality, banished from society, while infidelity, immodesty, and every other vice, stalked abroad with impunity. What then was his astonishment, on his arrival, to behold numbers of persons, both men and women, singularly devoted to exercises of piety! When Lent came round, the fast was strictly observed, fervent prayers were offered up at every altar, crowds flocked on pilgrimages from church to church, the confessionals were thronged by devout penitents, public penances were performed with wonderful contrition—in fact, the whole scene was so edifying, that he could not fancy anything more perfect. But when Holy Week arrived, the fervour of the preceding season was thrown into the shade by the great increase of devotion and penance. Prayers, corporal austerities. vigils, fasts, were all multiplied and performed with the most rigorous severity; worldly thoughts and occupations were banished, and the whole city was absorbed in the contemplation of the Crucified Saviour. So striking was the spectacle that Rome presented, that he could only exclaim, that words failed him to express, on the one hand, his detestation of the malice which, as he believed, had so calumniated the inhabitants of the Holy City, and, on the other, his admiration of the wonderful works of piety and penance which he himself witnessed.

And now if we pause to inquire who was the master-spirit that stirred and guided this mighty movement in Rome, both Catholics and Protestants will tell us that it was St. Philip. He entered Rome a mere youth, unknown, poor, and friendless; before he dies, by the mere force of the supernatural gifts of the Holy Ghost, he has changed the face of the city, and has rendered its population worthy of being the inhabitants of the centre of Christendom. He was called the Apostle of Rome, because he converted the

Romans to a life of the perfect love of God. He had no share in the government of the Church, no influence upon the policy of the Holy See, except in the one most characteristic instance of the absolution of Henry IV, which Baronius accomplished after his death. Yet he had a great influence in the Papal court, by promoting the individual holiness of its members. Cardinals and prelates were his penitents. The gentle flame of love went through and through the city. Shoemakers and soldiers, commercial clerks and bankers, sat side by side with lords temporal and spiritual on the benches of the Oratory, and Roman princesses and marchionesses elbowed the wives and daughters of tradesmen around his confessional. Who were all these, whose hearts Philip kindled with the tenderest love of God? They were the descendants of those Romans who had for ages been the most troublesome opponents of the Holy See. The spirit of God had given Philip a very outpouring of miraculous and supernatural powers, for the purpose of turning the mediæval Christian into something more resembling the Christian of the first ages of the Church. Among his spiritual children, you find some, like Nero dei Neri, whose names figured among the Guelf or Ghibelline nobles of the middle ages. The once turbulent Massimi were his most devoted friends. What would the fierce Sciarra Colonna, who insulted Boniface VIII at Anagni, have said if he had seen in spirit his descendants kneeling around Philip's confessional? Anna, the daughter-in-law of the Colonna who received the consecrated banner from the hands of St. Pius before he departed to command the papal galleys at Lepanto, was Philip's penitent and many casual notices in his life prove that this was only a specimen of Philip's work among the families of the once turbulent barons of Rome. All the Popes and Cardinals whom we have just mentioned, were his intimate friends. He sent so many novices to the Jesuits, that

St. Ignatius used to call him the bell of the Society, because, like a church bell, he called others to enter, while he himself remained outside. St. Camillus of Lellis, was his penitent, and Enrico Pietra was one of the young men out of the drapers' shops, whom he induced to take holy orders. St. Charles Borromeo and the Venerable Giovanni Leonardi submitted to him the rules of their respective institutes. The Barnabites would accept no novices who had not first been approved by him. If we glance over his memoirs, we shall find the names of saints and cardinals, of princes and prelates, of every well-known Roman family, mingling with those of lower degree down to the artisan, the decayed tradesman, and the destitute poor; so that it may be safely affirmed that, there was not a single individual of any note—one might almost say, not a single inhabitant of the city—who did not at some time or other come in contact with him. To this mixed multitude, the exercises of the Oratory, the daily sermons, the pilgrimages to the Seven Churches, and, above all, the influence of his own joyous, pure, and loving spirit, were as the dropping of water on the stony rock, or the genial dew on a barren soil, or as the heavenly leaven cast into the bosom of the population, and working there insensibly till the whole was leavened. What centuries had failed to perform, what force could never have effected, was now accomplished by the mighty power of supernatural love, and Rome was Christianized as it had never been before.

St. Philip Neri's tomb
Chiesa Nuova

CHAPTER XXVII

HILIP was now so old and feeble, he took so little nourishment, and he had besides such frequent attacks of severe illness, that it was no small subject of wonder to those around him how his life was prolonged. His very existence seemed scarcely less supernatural than the character of his life itself; for while, on the one hand, his body was consumed and worn out by the fervour of his spirit, so that he appeared to be languishing and dying of very love, yet, on the other, that undying spirit burnt so brightly in that poor feeble body, that it seemed as if it would not let it die. His tottering limbs would no longer support him without the aid of a stick, and yet there was a firm and cheerful tone in his sweet voice, and a joyful brightness in his eye which plainly told that his spirit was untouched by age, but that, in the words of the Psalmist: "his youth was renewed as the eagle's."

On his removal to the Vallicella, he had chosen for himself a room at the top of the house, furthest removed from accidental interruptions, and there he continued to live, so to speak, in a holy solitude, spending in prayer and contemplation all the time which was not given to the care of souls. His mornings were passed in the confessional, in which, notwithstanding his age and feebleness, he was as indefatigable as if he had been a young man just ordained. He set his sons a pattern of obedience and the love of poverty; for he would quit every other occupation the moment the sacristan called him to say Mass; and when he reached the sacristy, he would constantly say: "Give me the oldest and shabbiest vestments." He ruled by the spirit of love alone, feeling for each of his sons a more than father's tenderness, and leading them on in every word and action with such gentleness and sweetness, that their hearts were daily more and more inflamed with the love of God, so that words would fail to tell how light and easy he made the yoke of Christ to them. Though the fathers had elected him perpetual superior, yet he would not take that title, nor allow others to give it to him, and would never let himself be called by any other name than that of father. Hence it has become an established practice in all congregations of the Oratory of St. Philip, that the superior shall bear no other title than that of "the Father."

Each succeeding year he had his accustomed attacks of fever, and each attack revived the fears of his children, and spread alarm through Rome. In 1586, he was quite given up; but all on a sudden he was restored to his usual health. Again in 1591 and 1592, he was dangerously ill, but on each occasion he recovered so suddenly that his physicians declared his cure to be miraculous; for they had left him at night at the point of death, and when they returned in the morning, they found him as if he had never been ill.

In the year 1590, Gregory XIV, in consideration of his age and extraordinary devotion, dispensed him from saying the office, and granted him the privilege of celebrating Mass in a private oratory adjoining his own room. He would not, however, avail himself of the above dispensation except when he was ill, but continued till his death to say his office daily; though such was his constant state of extraordinary union with God, that he was obliged to say it with one of the fathers, because, if he said it alone, he would become abstracted as soon as he began, and would be unable to proceed. He, however, gladly availed himself of the privilege of saying his Mass in private, as it gave him the greater liberty to indulge his devotion, which was now so fervent that it could not be repressed. As soon as he came to the Agnus Dei, the server would light a small lamp, extinguish the candles on the altar, close the shutters, and leave the oratory, locking both doors and hanging over them a tablet with the words "Silence! the Father is saying Mass," so that none might intrude on that mysterious privacy. After two hours he would return and knock at the door, and if he received an answer, he would enter, relight the candles, and Philip would resume his Mass; but if, as it often happened, there was no answer, he would go away and return again after a time, never venturing to enter till he obtained permission to do so. Words cannot tell what passed during that mysterious interval between Philip and his Lord.

Many saints have had a miraculous devotion to the Blessed Sacrament, but there never was such a daily wonder upon earth as Philip's Mass. It was a glimpse of Paradise to see the old man with his countenance like an angel's, and his body buoyant like a spirit, and his eyes full of heavenly light, fixed upon his God and Saviour lying on a corporal before him. And when Mass was over his features seemed transparent, and his very soul shone through his white and wan face, as he walked back exhausted to his room.

As year after year passed by, Philip felt an increasing repugnance to holding the office of superior, and he often entreated the fathers to let him resign it, reminding them that death was drawing near, and that he needed leisure and retirement to make his preparations. The fathers, however, would not listen to his proposal, for the nearer his death approached, the less willing were they to anticipate by a single day the sorrowful period when another would have to take his place. Philip, therefore, had recourse to Cardinal Agostino Cusano and Cardinal Frederic Borromeo, both of whom had long been his penitents, requesting them to use their influence in his behalf. Accordingly, on the 7th July, A.D. 1593, the two cardinals addressed the assembled fathers, entreating them to let Philip resign, and to elect Baronius in his stead, and assuring them that this was also the wish of his Holiness Clement VIII. The fathers were most reluctant to take this step, and Baronius protested vehemently against his own election; but they saw they could no longer oppose the wishes of their Father, supported as they were by those of the Pope; and accordingly Philip resigned the superiorship, to which Baronius was unanimously elected. He held the office for three years till A.D. 1596, when, having been made cardinal, he resigned it, and Father Angelo Velli was elected to succeed him.

In April of the following year, A.D. 1594, Philip had a more than usually severe attack of fever, which lasted twenty-five days; in addition to which he was seized, in the month of May, with an acute pain in his loins, which was so violent that he could neither eat nor sleep, and in a few days he was reduced to the last extremity. Notwithstanding his great sufferings he preserved his usual cheerfulness and peace of mind, never uttering a word of complaint, but only saying very frequently in a low voice: "*Adauge dolorem, sed adauge patientiam.*"[29] At last, one afternoon, his physicians, Angelo da Bagnarea and Ridolfo Silvestri, came to see him, and found him with hardly any pulse, and so weak that he could scarcely move or speak; whereupon, seeing that there was no further hope, they drew the curtains of his bed, and stood aside in a corner of the room with Alessandro Alluminati, Antonio Gallonio, and Francesco Zazzara, who were watching by him, and were inconsolable to hear that their father was dying.

But while they were thus waiting in silence for his last breath, all on a sudden Philip cried out in a loud voice: "He

---

[29] "Intensify the suffering, but intensify patience." -Editor.

who desires anything but God deceives himself; and he who loves anything but God errs miserably," repeating the same words several times. On hearing him cry out thus, they all ran to the bedside, and drew the curtains, when, to their great wonder and awe, they beheld him raised up about a palm from the bed, and suspended in the air without any support, while at the same time he was stretching out his arms, as if he were embracing some object visible to himself alone, exclaiming in a clear voice, with tears of joy and affection: "Oh, my dearest Lady! Art thou come to free me from pain? Oh, most beautiful, most pure Virgin! Who am I that I should be found worthy of thy presence? No, certainly, no; I do not deserve such a favour. There is nothing good in me. Oh, blessed Virgin! what could induce thee to love me? I am quite unworthy of being visited by thee. Why, then, oh, most holy Virgin! dost thou come to me, the least of thy servants?" Then moving his arms, as if he were embracing the Queen of Heaven, he added: "Oh, most holy Mother of God! Oh, my beautiful Lady! Oh, most blessed Virgin! Oh, Mother of God! Why dost thou come to me? I shall then embrace thee since thou hast been pleased to grant me such a favour." He continued thus in ecstasy for a long time, calling on our Lady, and weeping profusely, till at last, as if returning to himself he said to those around: "Have you not seen the Mother of God who has come to visit me, and has freed me from pain?" And then looking round, and perceiving that so many persons were present, he hid his face in the bedclothes, and, bursting into tears, continued for a considerable time to weep audibly. At length the physicians, fearing that this emotion would exhaust him, tried to calm him; but he answered them plainly: "I have no more need of you; for our blessed Lady has been here, and has cured me." On hearing this, they felt his pulse, and found, indeed, as he had said, that the fever had left him, and that he was quite well. Though he earnestly besought all who were present not to mention what had happened, yet, no sooner did they leave his room, than they related it to all whom they met, so that it quickly spread through Rome. As soon as the news reached the Cardinals Cusano and Borromeo, they hastened to congratulate him, and he, knowing what pleasure the recital would give them, was at last induced to tell them all the particulars, which they at once transmitted to the Pope. To all who came to see him that evening he recommended great devotion to our Lady, expressing himself with the deepest emotion and tenderest affection, and saying: "Believe me, my sons, for I know it, that there is no more powerful means for obtaining favours from God than our blessed Lady."

During the remainder of the year 1594, Philip continued in his usual health. On the 30th of March, 1595, he had a very violent attack of fever, which confined him to his bed through the whole month of April. He, however, prayed our Lord as a special favour, to be enabled to say Mass on the 1st May, the feast of the Apostles St. Philip and St. James, and his prayer was granted; for he rose that morning from his bed, and said Mass, and gave Holy Communion to several of his penitents, though at the same time he was so weak that it was only a supernatural strength which carried him through. The next three days he abstained from saying Mass, in obedience to the physicians; but on the 5th May they gave him permission to celebrate, and he continued to do so daily till the 12th. On the morning of the 12th he was seized with such a violent flow of blood from his mouth that his pulse was gone, and he lay as if he were dead, while the physicians gave no hope of his recovery. As it seemed that each moment would be his last, Baronius gave him extreme unction, after which he seemed to revive a very little, and the physicians thinking he was then in a state to receive the

Viaticum, Cardinal Frederic Borromeo went to bring it him. But scarcely had he re-entered the room, bearing the Blessed Sacrament in his hand, than Philip, who till then had lain speechless and motionless in the last stage of exhaustion, seemed, to the astonishment of all around, to be recalled to life by the approach of his Lord; and beginning to weep, he cried out in a loud voice: "Here is my Love! Here is my Love! Here is my Beloved! Give Him to me quickly! Give Him to me quickly!" And when the cardinal, as he was about to communicate him, said: "Domine non sum dignus," he replied, in the most impassioned tone: "No, Lord, I am not worthy, nor ever was I worthy, for I have never done any good;" and as soon as he had communicated, he exclaimed: "Behold, now I have received my Physician!"

The same evening he had two or three returns of hemorrhage, accompanied with cough and great difficulty of breathing; but though he suffered a great deal, his sufferings made no impression on him, so great was his desire to shed not only the blood which came from his mouth, but every drop of blood in his veins, for love of that Lord who had so lovingly shed even to the last drop of His precious blood for him and for all mankind. Raising his eyes to heaven, he exclaimed: "God be praised that I can in any way give blood for blood;" and at another time perceiving that one of his sons looked pale and alarmed, he turned to him with a joyful countenance and said: "Are you afraid? I have not the least fear." And in fact this was only what he had often longed for, as some little compensation for being denied the privilege of shedding his blood in martyrdom. The usual remedies were applied, but none of them had the least effect.

On the following morning, however, when his physicians came to see him, he accosted them with the words: "Go you away, for my medicines are much better than yours. Very early this morning I sent alms to several religious houses, bidding them say Mass and pray for me, and forthwith the flow of blood and difficulty of breathing ceased; and now I feel so well that I think I am cured." And so indeed he was; for when the physicians had felt his pulse, and had examined him, they declared that he was quite recovered, and they gave him leave to get up. He had no further return of illness, but he said Mass daily, and heard confessions as usual; so that his children rejoiced to think that the danger was past, and that God was going to leave him with them for some time longer.

Philip too rejoiced, though in a far different way, for he knew that his hour was come, and that our Lord was about to call him to Himself and to crown him with glory in Paradise. He did not say much to his children about his approaching departure; but when he was gone, they recalled many words of his which plainly proved that the hour of his death had been revealed to him.

In all his preceding illnesses, he had been in the habit of making resolutions, in case of his recovery, to amend his life; but on this last occasion he seemed to have reached the perfection of humility in the full knowledge of his own nothingness; for he now only said: "Lord, if I get well, so far as depends on myself I shall always go on doing worse and worse; for I have so many times promised to change my life, and have never done it, that I have no longer any hopes of myself."

The day after his illness began, being the 31st March, he had a letter written to Father Flaminio Ricci, whom he tenderly loved, and who was then at Naples, ordering him to return to Rome as quickly as possible; and Father Ricci having replied, that for certain good reasons he could not come before September, he sent him another summons to come immediately. But the archbishop raising some difficulties about Ricci's departure, Philip had him again written to, no less than twice, remarking, however, on the last occasion: "He will not now be in time;" and so it came to pass, for when Father Ricci reached Rome, Philip was gone.

During the time that he had the hemorrhage, the Abate Marco Antonio Maffa said to him: "Never fear, father; God will let you live for a long time yet, if for nothing else, yet at least for the good of souls." But he answered with a smile: "If you manage to make me pass this year, what fine thing shall I give you?"

Twelve days before his death, Nero dei Neri having congratulated him on his recovery, he answered: "My Nero, I am cured, and at present I do not feel the least ill; but I tell you that within a few days I shall die; and when I die, no one will be expecting it, and my death will take place between light and dark," as indeed was the case.

Three years before, he had promised Francesco Zazzara, then a youth of eighteen, that he would tell him before he died what he was to do after his death; and Francesco used often to remind him of his promise, but Philip always answered: "Wait patiently, for I pray for you every day at Mass, and I will tell you what Our Lord reveals to me, so you need not fear that I shall die without first letting you know what I want you to do; for you have confided yourself to me, and I will not deceive you." During all this time, notwithstanding his frequent and alarming attacks of illness, he never said anything to Francesco but now, nine days before his death, he called him, and told him all that he had promised, whereupon Francesco could not help weeping, for he rightly judged that Philip's death was close at hand.

Ten days before his death, he called Giovan Battista Guerra, one of the brothers of the congregation, and said to him: "What day of the month is it?" Whereupon after

Battista answered that it was the 15th he rejoined: "Fifteen and ten make twenty-five, and after that we shall go."

On the vigil of Corpus Christi he sent for Father Pietro Consolini, and making him put his hand on his side, and feel his broken ribs, he said to him: "You will say Mass for me?" to which Consolini answered that he had already said it, and that when he had no other obligation he always said it for him; adding: "but I do not know that you have any need for it now, as you are recovered." But Philip replied: "The Mass I am asking for, is not one of those, but a Mass for the dead."

At last the feast of Corpus Christi, that most glorious feast in the year, arrived. Philip began the day by hearing the confessions of his spiritual children, and it was afterwards remarked that in so doing he had begged some of them to say a rosary or some other prayer for him after his death, that he had given each some solemn injunction respecting his future life, especially exhorting them to frequent the Sacraments, and to hear sermons, and to read the lives of the saints, and that he had taken leave of them all with demonstrations of more than usual affection. After the confessions were over, he said his office with great devotion, and then prepared to celebrate Mass. For some time past he had said his Mass with such extraordinary joyousness, that one might easily have known that his hour was at hand; but, on this morning, knowing that it was his last, he seemed to be carried quite beyond himself. As he was about to begin he looked fixedly towards Mount Onofrio, which was in sight, and thus he remained for a time gazing and abstracted, as if he beheld some great sight; and when he came to the Gloria he began to sing, and sang it through to the end with a fervour of joy and tenderness so unearthly, that it could be compared to nothing except the songs of the Angelic Hosts.

The rest of the day he spent in hearing the confessions

of a great number of his children, and in spiritual conversation with those who came to see him; and as they went away he took leave of them with peculiar tenderness, as if he knew that it was the last time he should see them. He had the life of St. Bernardino of Siena read to him, and when they came to the death of the saint, he made them read that part twice over. Late in the afternoon, Cardinal Cusano, who had already been with him earlier in the day, came again to see him, and with him and some others who happened to be present, he said the matins for the following day, this being the last portion of the office which he ever said on earth. After matins were finished, he went into an adjoining room, and the cardinal wishing to help him to ascend some steps, he laughed and said: "Do you think I am not strong?" Whereupon Angelo da Bagnarea, his physician, rejoined: "Father, you are better than ever. For the last ten years I have not seen you in such good health as to-day." After this, he heard Cardinal Cusano's confession; and in taking leave of him accompanied him, contrary to his usual custom, to the top of the stairs, pressing his hand warmly, and fixing his eyes affectionately on him, as if he would have said: "We shall not see each other again." After Cardinal Cusano's departure, he went on hearing confessions till supper time.

He supped as usual, and after supper, he heard the confessions of the fathers who were to say the first Masses next morning. Then many of the congregation came as usual to receive his blessing, and he gave it to them, conversing with them with indescribable sweetness and tenderness till three o'clock at night,[30] when he performed his accustomed

---

[30] In Italy the hours are numbered from the evening Angelus, which rings at sunset. In the month of May, three o'clock would correspond to between ten and eleven o'clock with us; and six o'clock, just after which Philip expired, would be between one and two o'clock in the morning.

devotions, and went to bed in perfect health. But knowing that his hour was close at hand, as soon as he lay down in bed, he uttered once more in a tone of solemn earnestness his oft-repeated words: "Well, at last we must die." Soon after he inquired what hour it was, and being told that three o'clock had just struck, he rejoined, as if speaking to himself: "Three and two are five, three and three are six, and after that we shall go." He then dismissed all who were with him, wishing to be left alone, in order to spend the little time which yet remained to him in sweet communion with his Lord, whose coming he was so joyfully awaiting. Soon after five o'clock, Father Antonio Gallonio, who slept in the room beneath his, heard him get up and walk about, and he instantly went to see what was the matter, when he found that he had thrown himself on his bed, and that his throat was so full of blood, that he seemed to be in danger of suffocating.

Gallonio asked him how he was, and he answered: "I am going." Gallonio then ran for assistance, and sent off for the physicians, and when he returned, accompanied by several of the other fathers, they found Philip sitting up in bed, in which posture he remained till he expired. They hoped it was only a return of the former hemorrhage, and they hastened to apply all the usual remedies; and in about a quarter of an hour, their fears began to subside, for the blood ceased to flow, he spoke freely and easily, and he seemed to be restored to his usual state. But Philip, unwilling that they should cherish so false a hope, said to them: "Do not trouble yourselves with any more remedies, for I am dying." These were his last words. After this he spoke no more, but closing his eyes, he seemed to retire within himself, listening in his heart for the voice of his Lord when He should call him, and thus preparing himself to meet with firmness the last struggle with Death. Meanwhile, the fathers had all been summoned, and they assembled in haste, weeping bitterly, as well they might for the loss of such a father; and Philip seemed to await their coming, as if he were unwilling to depart till they were all there. At length they had all arrived, and were kneeling in anguish round the bed, and Baronius had made the recommendation of the soul, when the physician, feeling his pulse, said that he was going. Then Baronius, turning to him, cried out in a loud voice: "Father, are you going without saying anything to us? At least, give us your blessing." On hearing these words, Philip opened his eyes, and casting them up to heaven, remained for a short time thus, after which, looking down upon his children, he seemed as if he would say that he had prayed to God for them. Then, without a sigh or a struggle, he expired, gently and peacefully as if he were falling asleep.

During the course of the night the fathers dressed Philip's body in the priestly vestments, and carried it down in solemn procession to the church, where they laid it on a bier. Early next morning the news of his death spread abroad, and crowds of people of all ranks and ages, cardinals, archbishops, prelates, and religious of every order and every grade, princes, nobles, and high-born ladies, rich and poor, young and old, priests and laymen, all pressed to gaze for the last time on him who was so dear to every heart in Rome.

Such was the veneration which they felt for the saint that they would not stand in his presence, but threw themselves prostrate before him; they kissed his hands and feet, or the bier on which he lay; they touched his body with their rosaries; they carried off the roses which had been thrown on the corpse, seizing them with such eagerness that the fathers could not supply them fast enough; nay, some even dared, with loving boldness, to cut off pieces of his habit and locks of his hair, which they bore away with fond devotion, and treasured up as precious relics. It was a touching sight to witness that great, mixed, sorrowing crowd, united in one common grief, weeping over the bier of their father, and he lying there with his own sweet smile, looking calm and loving, as if he were still among them. As for his own penitents, they could never be satisfied with gazing at him; in vain would they summon resolution to take their last look; for still they must have another look, and then another, so that the longer they gazed, the more impossible did they find it to tear themselves from the spot.

During the following night the body was opened in the presence of the first physicians of Rome; and then was seen, what has been already told, that the swelling which had existed since the day when he had so miraculously received the Holy Spirit, was caused by two of the ribs over the heart being broken and elevated in the form of an arch. It was no small subject of wonder to the physicians that the ribs should never have reunited, and that he should have lived thus for above fifty years without suffering any pain; and, after careful examination and consultation, they affirmed, in writing and on oath, that the case was supernatural and miraculous, and the only explanation they could suggest, was that God had made this special provision for the extraordinary palpitations of his heart, to which he had ever after been subject.

After three days his body was buried under the high altar, on the epistle side, in the place which had been prepared for him when the church was built. But when Cardinal Frederic Borromeo and Cardinal Alessandro de' Medici heard where he had been laid, it seemed to them that so great a saint should have some more distinguished burying-place; and accordingly, at their request, he was removed, on the following day, to a small chapel, above the first arch of the nave of the church, on the epistle side.

Though he had been so long dead, yet his limbs were found to be soft and flexible, and his countenance wore the same grave and dignified expression as in life; and, neither at this time, nor when the body was opened, was the least unpleasant smell perceptible. All the circumstances of his interment and subsequent removal had been predicted by himself. For one day, when Giovan Battista Guerra was telling him what arrangements had been made for the burial of the members of the congregation, and that his place was on the epistle side of the high altar, he said,—"You will not leave me there." To which Guerra replied: "Yes, father, we shall." But Philip rejoined,—"I tell you that you will put me there, but you will not leave me there." And on another occasion he told Father Francesco Bozzio that he would come and take up his abode near him; and Father Bozzio objecting that the room next to his was not good enough for him, he still insisted that he would do so. All this came literally to pass. For it was Giovan Battista Guerra who laid Philip's body under the high altar, and he removed it the next day to the chapel above mentioned, which was close to Father Bozzio's room.

Nearly four years after, A.D. 1599, Nero dei Neri undertook to build a magnificent chapel for Philip's remains, but the fathers thought it desirable, in the first place, to examine the body, in order to ascertain whether it was in a fit state for removal. Accordingly, on the 7th March, the wall was removed, and the coffin was examined, when it was found that, in consequence of the damp, the lid of the coffin had decayed, and the cloths and other coverings were so completely gone that they fell to pieces as soon as they were touched; but when all the coverings had been removed, to their great joy it appeared that the body had undergone little change, but looked almost as fresh as when they had laid it there, and no disagreeable smell proceeded either from it or from the pieces of cloth which had lain on it in a state of decay. The body was now placed in a new coffin, the chapel was at once commenced, and on the 24th May, A.D. 1602, it was removed thither with the usual solemnities.

It was only to be expected that one whose life on earth had been a course of miracles, should continue to exercise the same supernatural power after his removal to the presence of God. Scarcely then was Philip dead, than his relics were eagerly sought, his name was fervently invoked, and vows were made to his honour, while volumes would not suffice to record all the favours which were thus obtained. From the period of his death up to the present time, a continuous chain of miracles attests his sanctity; and many living witnesses can now be found to declare the wonders which they either have themselves experienced, or have beheld in others. But though no one doubted that Philip was a saint, yet the Church is so cautious as regards those whom she places on her altars, that previous to his canonization, the deeds which had been wrought in the midst of Rome and before the whole city, were required to be juridically proved on oath by eye-witnesses, and the evidence was subjected to scrutiny far surpassing in severity that of any other tribunal; and thus many years elapsed before the necessary forms could be gone through. At length, however, during the pontificate of Gregory XV, on the 12th March, A.D. 1622, being the feast of St. Gregory the Great, his canonization was solemnized in St. Peter's, and as if to shed greater honour on the occasion, his name was united with those of St. Ignatius, St. Francis Xavier, St. Theresa, and St. Isidore.

It is the privilege of the saints to live and speak even after their death, and with none is this more plainly seen to be the case than with St. Philip. He who walks through Rome at the present day, may hear St. Philip's name invoked with loving familiarity, as if every Roman knew him personally and felt him to be his father; and even in colder climes, St. Philip's children may be recognized by the familiar fondness with which they cherish his name and his memory. Other saints have bequeathed a code of laws to their children, but St. Philip's law was love; and hence, the inheritance which he has left as an heirloom to his children, is the spirit of love; so that after the lapse of well nigh three centuries, St. Philip's children, whatever be their birth, their language, or their clime, continue to yield him the same free and loving obedience as when he was among them, making his words and wishes the guide of their actions, and dwelling together in fraternal affection, with no other union than love to their common father, and no other bond than love to Him, who is Himself Infinite and Substantial Love.

FINIS

Other books you may like from Mediatrix Press:

Cesar Cardinal Baronius: Founder of Church History
Brother Deo Gratias: The Life of St. Francis of Cantalice
A Capuchin Chronicle
The Life of St. Francis of Assisi
St. John Capistrano: A Reformer in Battle
The Autobiography of St. Charles of Sezze
As the Morning Star: The Life of St. Dominic
Dominican Life
St. Albert the Great: The First Universal Doctor
St. Dominic's Successor: Blessed Jordan of Saxony
The Spiritual Life and Prayer according to Scripture and Monastic Tradition
The Public Life of Our Lord Jesus Christ (2 vols)
St. John Fisher: Reformer, Humanist, Martyr
St. Thomas More: A Great Man in hard times
The Life of the Venerable Anne of Jesus
The Sermons of the Cure of Ars
The Life of Pope Leo XIII
St. Thérèse and the Faithful

For these and more, visit us at:
www.mediatrixpress.com

CPSIA information can be obtained
at www.ICGtesting.com
Printed in the USA
LVHW080153270522
719908LV00011B/678